Great Basin Rock Art

Great Basin Rock Art

Archaeological Perspectives

EDITED BY **ANGUS R. QUINLAN**

UNIVERSITY OF NEVADA PRESS RENO & LAS VEGAS

University of Nevada Press, Reno, Nevada 89557 USA
New material copyright © 2007
by University of Nevada Press

Manufactured in the United States of America
Library of Congress Cataloging-in-Publication Data
Great Basin rock art : archaeological perspectives /
edited by Angus R. Quinlan.
p. cm.
Includes bibliographical references and index.
ISBN-13: 978-0-87417-696-4 (hardcover : alk. paper)
1. Indians of North America—Great Basin—Antiquities.
2. Rock paintings—Great Basin. 3. Petroglyphs—Great
Basin. 4. Great Basin—Antiquities.
I. Quinlan, Angus R., 1968–
E78.G67G74 2006
979'.01—DC22   2006023848

The paper used in this book is a recycled stock made
from 50 percent post-consumer waste materials and
meets the requirements of American National Standard
for Information Sciences—Permanence of Paper for
Printed Library Materials, ANSI Z39.48–1984. Binding
materials were selected for sgtrength and durability.

First Printing
15   14   13   12   11   10   09   08   07   06
5   4   3   2   1

"The Study of a Rock Art Site in Southeastern Oregon"
by Keo Boreson is a heavily revised version of a report
compiled under contract with the U.S. Bureau of Reclamation.

Contents

Illustrations

TABLES

Preface

This book is a collection of essays by twelve scholars that explores Great Basin rock art from an archaeological perspective. The goal of the volume is to show how archaeology has helped us understand the meaning and purpose of rock art in the daily lives of the Great Basin's indigenous peoples. In the past decade, the archaeological examination of the physical environment and cultural associations of rock art has provided some important insights into the social context of this enigmatic art form. In addition, rock art has a contemporary cultural resonance to Native American peoples (its traditional custodians) and is of considerable interest to the general public. These contemporary contexts of rock art's use-life are also explored in this volume and illustrate how interpretation, heritage conservation, and professional research are intertwined.

The essays were inspired by a session presented at the 2002 Biennial Great Basin Anthropological Conference in Elko, Nevada. The session, which was organized by Alanah Woody and sponsored by the Nevada Rock Art Foundation and the Nevada State Museum, explored archaeology's role in constructing rock art's contemporary heritage value, as well as the kinds of interpretations popularly presented to the public. The Nevada Rock Art Foundation and the Nevada State Museum are committed to the preservation of Nevada's (and more generally the Great Basin's) archaeological heritage. They sponsor programs of public and professional interpretation to raise awareness of heritage issues (thereby building community capacity), as well as fostering professional debate to develop archaeological research. It is a pleasure to acknowledge their role in providing the original venue for the research and ideas expressed in this book.

Angus R. Quinlan
Minden, 2005

Acknowledgments

Editor: The development of the essays in this book benefited greatly from the insightful commentary and review by the original session discussant, Catherine S. Fowler. The editorial staff of the University of Nevada Press, particularly Margaret Dalrymple, were always helpful and supportive. The manuscript was thoughtfully and thoroughly copyedited by Jan McInroy; Ralph Bennett prepared for publication the illustrations in chapters 6 and 7. Last, I thank my wife, Alanah Woody, for all her hard work on this volume, as well as for her support and patience.

Chapter 5: Signa Pendegraft thanks Ted Goebel, Alvin McLane, Angus Quinlan, Mary Rusco, and Alanah Woody for their help with this project.

Chapter 7: Keo Boreson gratefully acknowledges the efforts of the personnel of the U.S. Bureau of Reclamation, Snake River Office (particularly Ray Leicht), who made this project happen. She also thanks Ryan Ives, Pam McKinney, Joe Randolph, and Ann Sharley-Hubbard, who participated in the fieldwork, and all of her coworkers at Archaeological and Historical Services who helped with all aspects of the project.

Chapter 9: Eric Ritter, Alanah Woody, and Alan Watchman were assisted in the field by James Barnes and Julie Burcell of the BLM. Funding for this project was provided by the Bureau of Land Management, the James W. Calhoun Foundation, and the Nevada State Museum. Ann McNichol and Susan Handwork at the National Ocean Sciences Accelerator Mass Spectrometry Facility, Woods Hole, Massachusetts, assisted with sample preparation and analysis of the small varnish samples. Watchman is supported by an Australian Research Council Fellowship and a grant to investigate the nature and age of organic matter in rock surface coatings.

Great Basin Rock Art

CHAPTER 1

Integrating Rock Art with Archaeology

Symbolic Culture as Archaeology

ANGUS R. QUINLAN

Rock art is currently enjoying something of a boom in public and archaeological interest, although in North America its study and practice still
occur predominantly outside the world of academic and professional
archaeology. Only a handful of doctoral dissertations are written each year
on the subject. It is largely absent from academic curricula, and only a very
small number of professional archaeologists specialize in it. Symptomatic
of this professional disinterest and neglect is the large number of amateur
archaeologists who make important contributions to the study of rock
art, despite lacking formal qualifications in archaeology or anthropology.
In some regards this situation mirrors the early history of archaeology
as a discipline, when amateurs dominated the field and the subject was
entirely absent from university campuses. Yet archaeology's exclusion
from academia was relatively brief compared to that of rock art, for the
exclusion of rock art studies from North American academic institutions
shows no immediate signs of ending—though there has been sporadic
archaeological interest since the days of Garrick Mallery (1893), and Great

Basin rock art attracted the attentions of no lesser a figure than Julian Steward (Steward 1929, 1937). Curiously, a critical retrospective of Julian Steward's career (Clemmer et al. 1999) mentions his engagement with rock art only in passing, as if it were a kind of hobby, separate from Steward's anthropological career.

The separation between academic archaeology and the study of rock art has had important consequences for the way in which the field is conceptualized and the state and quality of theory building. Rock art can appear to be highly distinct, its study demanding specialized interpretations and theories that have little purchase in other fields of archaeology. Rock art can be minimally defined as non-utilitarian intentional human-made markings on rock surfaces (Bednarik 2001:31–32), a definition incorporating paintings, engravings, and scratchings, made on boulders, rimrocks, cliff edges, and cave ceilings and walls. Thus, a rock art "site" is essentially a collection or assemblage of images made on natural rock surfaces.

Because of rock art's landscape context, its imagery has never been treated the same way as imagery placed in constructed structures. Instead, rock art has been treated rather like other non-utilitarian archaeology, as the residue of past ritual practice. Archaeological approaches to ritual are rarely explicit about how ritual spaces are identified. Those that have been explicit about their methodology have used the presence of symbolism to infer a ritual function for the archaeological contexts in which it occurs (Renfrew 1985:24). In such cases the objects identified as functioning as religious symbols (and thus as an index of ritual practice) tend to be non-utilitarian (Quinlan 1993:98). Therefore, since rock art constitutes assemblages of symbolism, it is not surprising that it tends to be naturally associated with the spiritual sphere in archaeological thinking.

Reflecting this tendency, rock art (once its cultural authenticity was accepted) was first theorized as having being used in rituals of hunting magic (Breuil 1952; Heizer and Baumhoff 1959, 1962; Reinach 1903) and more recently as sources of shamanistic powers and records of trance states (Clottes and Lewis-Williams 1998; Lewis-Williams 2002; Lewis-Williams and Dowson 1988). Yet these theories are unique to rock art and have rarely been applied to other ritual contexts encountered by archaeologists (though for a recent attempt to extend the shamanistic model to other kinds of ritual archaeology, see Price 2001).

Although the defining property of rock art (imagery made on natural rock surfaces) is unique, in other regards it is not so divorced from other types of archaeology. In particular, the distribution of rock art is not always specialized, and it frequently occurs in association with settlement archaeology, such as lithic scatters, house rings, hunting blinds, and so on, as many of the chapters in this volume illustrate. Whether these other kinds of archaeology are considered an integral part of a rock art site depends to a large extent on the kind of theories we use to bring meaning to the residues of past behavior. For example, researchers working in the Great Basin have drawn rather different conclusions from rock art's associated archaeology. In the 1960s Heizer and Baumhoff's (1962) application of hunting magic theory to North America crucially used associated archaeology to demonstrate that rock art sites were present at hunting locales (evidenced by the association of rock art with hunting blinds, animal migratory routes, lithic scatters, and so on). In contrast, Whitley interprets rock art as a means of marking places where shamans made secret pilgrimages to acquire supernatural powers, and thus rock art is rarely associated with other kinds of archaeology (Whitley 1994a, 1994c, 1998c).

In both of these examples, the authors' interpretations of rock art's associated archaeology are determined by their preferred theoretical perspectives, which are challenged by the presence of domestic archaeology occurring in association with rock art (see chapters by Cannon and Woody, Pendegraft, Shock, and Cannon and Ricks in this volume). Consequently, the presence of settlement archaeology at rock art sites is downplayed so that the sites' properties accord with the theoretical expectation. As Cannon and Woody illustrate in chapter 4, this tendency is not confined to rock art specialists; archaeologists are just as likely to ignore rock art at settlement sites.

In both cases, although it is possible to gain some understanding of rock art simply by contemplating its imagery, broader considerations of site context offer more textured accounts of rock art's cultural meanings. Such an approach recognizes the importance of understanding and establishing context in archaeological interpretation (Hodder 1986:119–20) and the way in which context potentially represents an extension of symbolic meaning (Sperber 1975). Renewed interest in rock art's fuller context has produced an increase in studies that explore its landscape context as a source of cultural meaning (Bradley 1997, 2000; Tilley 1991). For example, Quinlan and Woody (2003) have attempted to reconstruct the social roles of Great Basin rock art sites by exploring the implications of their location in or near the routines of domestic life, a theme of several chapters in this volume. Such approaches shift the gaze away from rock art's imagery and treat it as a light source that can illuminate the social and cultural world of its makers (Sperber 1975:70), also avoiding some of the problems associated with an exclusive focus on recovering the "meaning" of ancient imagery, as illustrated by Maurice Bloch's cautionary tale of interpreting Zafimaniry (Madagascar) wood carvings: "To the question 'what are these pictures of' I was answered with great certainty that they were pictures of nothing. When I asked for a cause or the point of the carvings I triggered the ready-made phrase that there was no point, and when I asked what people were doing I was told 'carving.' There was actually one answer that I was given very often . . . that 'it made the wood beautiful'" (Bloch 1995:213–14).

Understanding Zafimaniry wood carvings is possible only through understanding the significance of the houses and the wood that the carvings decorate. The carvings are not representational but play a part in the process of a house, and the union between the married couple who dwell there, "hardening" or becoming increasingly solid and permanent in structure (Bloch 1995:214–15). In this case symbolism is important for what it actually does, a point made in rock art by the shamanistic approach, which considers some rock art as playing an active role in stimulating trance states (Lewis-Williams and Dowson 1990).

It is rock art's perceived relationship with past religious practices that partly explains its appeal to the general public and its professional neglect in North American archaeology. Emphasizing distinctive theories of ritual functions has led other archaeologists to believe that rock art has little to offer their fields of expertise and can be safely ignored. Further, archaeology's will to classification and quantification (which came to the fore in the New Archaeology of the 1960s and 1970s) made rock art a problematic field of archaeological inquiry, as its object of study resists easy classification and is hard to date (Woody 2000a:5–6).

The chapters in this volume reflect the growing confidence of rock art researchers that recent theoretical and methodological developments have made rock art's integration into broader archaeological research an achievable goal. Further, rock art researchers justifiably question why North American archaeology has ignored the most visible monument form left by Native Americans, which remains in the place where it was intended to be, in favor of, for example, studying lithic debitage. At last it seems that archaeologists are beginning to take up Julian Steward's injunction to "set aside their spades long enough to ponder petroglyphs" (1937:406).

The regional focus of this volume is predominantly the northern Great Basin and adjacent areas (figure 1.1), whose rock art has played an important role in international debates regarding the social and cultural contexts of its original use (Layton 2000b; Lewis-Williams and Dowson 1988; Whitley 1992). These debates have tended to focus on ethnography and ethnohistory rather than archaeological studies of the rock art itself. Consequently, the landscape context of Great Basin rock art has been inadequately reported. Several of the contributors whose work is included here (Boreson [chapter 7], Cannon and Ricks [chapter 8], Cannon and Woody [chapter 4], Pendegraft [chapter 5], and Shock [chapter 6]) address this deficit by exploring the relationships among rock art, landscape features, and settlement archaeology in this region, offering an important corrective to the misperception of rock art as a unique landscape monument with a specialized distribution and revealing significant implications for current theoretical debates.

At present rock art interpretation is dominated by approaches that seek to understand its imagery through the framework of ethnohistorical accounts (Francis and Loendorf 2002; Whitley 1992, 1994a, 2000a). Drawing on ethnographic accounts of traditional shamanic practices, such work interprets rock art as having being made and used by shamans in their pursuit and use of supernatural powers (spirit helpers). The argument posits that the art itself portrays specific imagery experienced during trance states. The value of this kind of approach is that it aims to include indigenous theories of being in the effort to understand rock art, assuming that traditional shamanic practices provide an informing context for the interpretation of rock art imagery. The approach is less useful, however, when it is based upon speculative reinterpretations of ethnographic material (for debate on the role of metaphoric reinterpretation of ethnographic data in rock art interpretation, see Hedges 2001; Quinlan 2000a, 2000b, 2001; Whitley 2000a, 2003).

Figure 1.1. Map of the Northern Great Basin and adjacent areas showing tribal territories and places mentioned in the text. After d'Azevedo 1986:ix

Such theoretically driven works offer specific interpretation of imagery, without necessarily reflecting on the art's landscape context and its role in adding to site meaning. Cannon and Ricks, Cannon and Woody, Pendegraft, and Shock, on the other hand, explore the interpretive implications of rock art's landscape context. These authors, drawing on their research from the northern Great Basin, highlight an often ignored property of western U.S. rock art locales: their location in or near the margins of settlement. They document a direct association between rock art and settlement archaeology in their study regions and argue that this challenges the simple assumption of shamanism as the primary informing context for interpretation. Landscape context discloses the character of rock art's intended audiences and suggests that the shamanic perspective needs to be complemented by interpretations that consider the domestic routines that took place in the vicinity of rock art (Bradley 2000; Quinlan and Woody 2003). This approach decenters the search for the meanings of motifs as *the* object of rock art research. Instead, by contextualizing the available informing contexts, these authors challenge popular interpretive theory and situate rock art in the domain of the lived experience of daily life.

Brown and Woody (chapter 2) and Valborg and Cunningham (chapter 3) address the issue of indigenous approaches to rock art, and archaeology more generally, and in differing ways look at the way Native Americans incorporate rock art into contemporary discourses of meaning. Brown and Cunningham are Native Americans, and their views are contrasted with those of their archaeologist coauthors. In the case of Brown and Woody, it is interesting that the indigenous preference is for Western science and Native American viewpoints to be used in a complementary way to support traditional views of the land's geological history. In the case of Valborg and Cunningham, the tension between archaeological and indigenous frames of understanding is highlighted, opening the question that confronts most researchers today of whether both of these ways of understanding rock art can be accommodated (Echo-Hawk 2000; Mason 2000). Further, Valborg and Cunningham illustrates the symbolic properties of the archaeological record in general—the same body of archaeological data sustains competing theories of being and constructions of cultural identity.

The reasons for rock art's appeal to the general public and its integration into contemporary material culture is an important issue that is neglected in the literature. When it is discussed (Dowson 1999), public consumption of rock art imagery through its reproduction in popular material culture (mugs, key chains, and so on) and coffee table books is strongly criticized as commodification. However, Quinlan balances this position by examining the role of archaeological research in making such commodification possible by creating a contemporary cultural value for rock art as well as providing the raw materials (photographs, drawings, and so on) used in rock art's commercial exploitation.

Finally, Boreson (chapter 7) and Ritter, Woody, and Watchman (chapter 9) provide accounts of direct dating studies and fieldwork methodology. They serve as an important reminder that interpretive debate can proceed only so long as archaeologists continue to set aside their spades and record rock art sites. With greater quality of information will come greater resolution in debate, allowing researchers to ask more challenging and appropriate questions of rock art.

PART I ETHNOGRAPHIC PERSPECTIVES

CHAPTER 2

Stories as Old as the Rocks

Rock Art and Myth

MELVIN BROWN AND ALANAH WOODY

In this chapter we discuss a pictograph site on the west side of Agai-Pah (Trout Lake) or Walker Lake, near the mouth of Copper Canyon on the east side of the Wassuk Range in western Nevada (see figure 1.1). The red iron oxide pictographs are found on the northwest face of an immense boulder (more than 3 meters high and 6 meters long) (figure 2.1). There are several other rock art sites in the general vicinity, but this is the only pictograph site currently known in the area. In the absence of indigenous exegesis, interpretation of rock art imagery can only be speculative. We attempt to contextualize our interpretation, however, by taking into account local oral tradition. Oral tradition has been broadly used in rock art research to offer insights into the meanings of images and theories about the functions of rock art (Lewis-Williams 1981; Vinnicombe 1976). One benefit of using oral tradition to contextualize interpretation is the possibility of capturing some of rock art's local cultural salience in the present as well as in the past. In the case of the Agai-Pah pictograph site, we relate it to Walker River Paiute (Northern Paiute) traditions of a sea serpent that dwelled in

Figure 2.1. The Agai-Pah Pictograph Site, Nevada, April 2005. Photograph by
A. Woody

Walker Lake. These oral traditions may represent folk memories of Walker
Lake flooding and observations of the fossil remains of ichthyosaurs. In
addition, the Agai-Pah site has meaning for Brown as a Walker River Paiute, since he interprets its placement and imagery as referring to flood
episodes detailed by geological research.

PREVIOUS REPORTS OF THE AGAI-PAH PICTOGRAPH SITE

The Agai-Pah pictograph site seems to have avoided the academic gaze
until the 1920s; it was not noted in Mallery's (1893) survey of rock art sites
and was also omitted from Steward's seminal study (1929). The first record
of the site dates from the 1920s, when it was used as a setting for one of
Edward Curtis's romantic photographs of traditional indigenous cultural
practices (1997 [1926]:588). The photograph is of a Native American man
with "loin cloth," moccasins, and paintbrush, supposedly in the process
of creating the art. This staged event used the pictograph panel on the
western face of the boulder as a backdrop to the portrait of the Native
American man. Whether or not Curtis also noticed or photographed the
north-facing group of pictographs is unknown. Subsequent observers

have concluded that the motifs "appear to be authentic, both stylistically and in their execution" (Tuohy 1983), making it unlikely that they were created by Curtis's subject.

Subsequently the site was reported in Heizer and Baumhoff's (1962) gazetteer of rock art sites (figure 2.2), although their drawing of the art is somewhat inaccurate. They commented on the boulder's dimensions, noted its location, and made a line drawing of part of the north-facet motifs and all of the west-facet ones. In the 1970s it appears that this pictograph panel was implicated in a hoax. Apparently a geologist who resided in the Hawthorne area was sold "Spanish treasure" excavated from the base of the pictograph boulder. The pictographs were supposedly a map to further buried Spanish silver. The "treasure" of Spanish coins, spurs, a bit, and silver bars was in fact base metals and plaster of Paris. Don Tuohy, of the Nevada State Museum, had the unpleasant task of informing the geologist that he had been duped (Tuohy 1983).

PICTOGRAPH CHARACTERISTICS

The red ochre pictographs are located on two sides of a very large granite boulder at the mouth of Copper Canyon; this boulder may have reached its current position as the result of flash flooding. The boulder is about 3 meters high, 6 meters long, and 0.3 meters wide. Perched on top is a smaller boulder (1.82 × 0.9 × 0.6 meters), and to the east is wedged another boulder (4.8 × 3 × 0.6 meters), but neither of these has rock art.

The pictographs are positioned on two facets of the boulder, to the north and west of a vertical ridge. The north-facet motif is very faint and comprises three joined rough triangular shapes with four lines radiating from its southwest apex. Discerning these motifs is difficult because of the effects of wind erosion and the subsequent deposition of a light film of iron oxide.

In contrast, the west-facet motifs are easier to see because the rock surface is smoother and less iron oxide has accumulated on it. At the bottom of the facet is a tubular shape ("fish" shape), which seems to be entering a larger Y-shaped motif. The Y-shaped motif is flanked by two circles, and immediately above are two lines of zigzags that seemingly divide the lower section of the panel from an upper circle that has six lines radiating from one half of it (see figure 2.2).

Figure 2.2. The Agai-Pah Pictographs, Nevada. After Heizer and Baumhoff 1962: figure 99b

Various interpretations of the pictographs have been suggested. Heizer and Baumhoff (1962:90) commented that "the painted figure seems to be swimming into the mouth of a stream." In 1977 a group of Walker River Paiute Tribal Elders conducted field trips to several nearby rock art sites; their report of these field trips contains the following description about the pictograph boulder: "The second field trip found the class at what is referred to as Serpent Rock. This huge boulder overlooks Walker Lake and depicts in red native paint, a fish, water waves, and what appears to be a water serpent. This site is also located at the ancient high water mark and at the mouth of the canyon where there is much evidence of flash flooding" (Agai-Ticutta [Walker River Paiute Tribe] 1977).

By referring to the site as "Serpent Rock" and interpreting its imagery in terms of water waves and a water serpent, the elders seem to be interpreting the rock art imagery in terms of local traditions of a great flood and a sea serpent. The tribal history of the Walker River Paiute contains a section about the Agai-Dicutta Tribal Legend of the Walker Lake Sea Serpent (Johnson 1975:182–87). It includes "eyewitness" accounts by Native Americans as well as local white residents. The local oral traditions obviously aroused the interest of whites, for they found their way into the local newspaper. A number of oral traditions tell of great sea serpents that live in Walker Lake. In one tradition, two serpents were human beings—a man and a woman—and children were instructed not to make fun of them or to talk lightly about them. Around the time Pleistocene Lake Lahontan receded, one of the pair died, and thereupon the surviving serpent crawled to Sand Mountain (east of Fallon) to die. The sound made today by the blowing sand is said to be the serpent crying for its lost mate. Another tradition records that a long time ago a man saw a monster lying on the western bank of the lake and shot arrows at it, but they just bounced off. He decided to heat his arrows, and then they pierced the monster. When he returned one year later he found ribs that were bigger than those of a cow (Johnson 1975:182–87).

These indigenous traditions of monster serpents dwelling in Walker Lake came to the attention of local newspapers (Johnson 1975:182–87). The *Walker Lake Bulletin* in 1883 reported that Native Americans who lived at the lake were awakened one night by the shrieking of two monster serpents fighting. The battle moved onto the land, and one of the serpents was seriously injured and then killed by people and given to a white man. Stories continued to be printed about the Walker Lake Serpent, and in 1907 Professor David Starr Jordan, president of Stanford University and the foremost ichthyologist of the time, planned to come to Walker Lake and capture the serpent for study. By that time white people had also begun to see the serpent with some regularity, and when the road beside the lake was constructed in the 1920s, numerous tourists driving between Hawthorne and the Schurz Indian Reservation reported seeing a huge monster swimming in the lake. In 1934 an article in the *Mineral County Independent* speculated that the serpent in Walker Lake may have traveled through an underground channel to Pyramid Lake, where it was believed another great serpent (named ANG) also dwelt. Apparently, the last published account of the serpent was in 1956, when the editor of the Hawthorne newspaper claimed that he and his wife watched something moving in the lake for fifteen minutes. Some newspaper reports were more skeptical—the editor of the *Lyon County Times* in 1907 wrote: "It is 25 or 26 years ago since we heard the story of the big snake in Walker Lake. It is an Indian story, pure and simple, and it may be possible that the Indians believe in it. From time to time of late years it is said that the serpent has been seen by white men, but the stories about its size and looks differ greatly. It is more than likely that what they have seen is [a] long line of swan or other water fowl, which abound on the lake, swimming on its surface" (Johnson 1975:183).

What can account for these stories? Are they all hoaxes? We believe that one explanation may be based on the fossil remains of ichthyosaurs that can be seen in some parts of Nevada (at Ichthyosaur State Park, Berlin, for example). Peoples in the past may have come to understand that these giant reptiles once lived in the area, but only their fossil remains could now be seen. Knowledge of the remains of these great reptiles may have come to personify an event that happened in the distant past. It is not uncommon for non-Western cultures to attribute personalized agency to natural phenomena.

There is evidence in the sediments of Walker Lake, or Agai-Pah, of a rapid filling that would have been witnessed by the people who lived there. Over time, the story would have been retold and altered to fit with other stories of long ago. The symbol of the fish, the fossil remains of ichthyosaurs, and the story of the flood combine to create the idea of a water serpent that went to live in Agai-Pah. We believe that the catastrophic event itself is embodied in the serpent described in the stories and depicted in the Walker Lake pictographs. If there indeed was widespread catastrophic flooding (ca. 4,700 years ago), descriptions of such an experience may have been recorded in oral traditions and passed down through the generations.

Brown believes that one reading of these Walker River Paiute traditions is that the concept of a water serpent filling the lake basin with *itself* functions as a metaphor for ancient flood episodes and that the traditions underwent changes through time—particularly with the adoption of certain Euro-American themes and concepts in indigenous thought—until the flood references became implicit rather than overt. Accordingly, Brown interprets the Agai-Pah pictograph motifs as describing parts of a flood story of Walker Lake. The Y-shaped motif is interpreted as a metaphoric reference to a step in willow preparation (Wheat 1967). Thus the fishlike motif (perhaps representing the flood water or even the sea serpent itself) that appears to be entering it is splitting the land "in a manner of splitting willow" (see figure 2.2). The circles represent the rock's eyes, watching or experiencing the arrival of rapid floodwaters. In addition, the circles constrict the Y shape in the manner of rocks funneling the passage of water. Immediately above are the paired zigzag lines, suggesting turbulent movement or sound, perhaps representing dispersing flash-flooding waters. Moving to the upper section, we see the constricted oval shape that implies easy separation (like manipulating clay). Above is the circle with radiating lines terminated by dots, interpreted as "going in many directions." On the north side of the boulder is a large shape that perhaps describes floodwaters from the north (this shape looks like a larger quadruped or animal, or may even represent the Walker sea serpent itself).

GEOLOGICAL CHARACTERISTICS OF THE SITE

This reading of the Agai-Pah pictograph boulder and Walker River Paiute traditions as referring to flood episodes finds some basis in geological evidence for such flooding in the past, and illustrates that traditional knowledge is not simply symbolic.

The Agai-Pah pictograph boulder is located near the mouth of Copper Canyon, on the west side of Walker Lake, and may have been deposited there as the result of flooding. Looking west from the boulder toward Copper

Canyon, one sees a terrace that was created by continuous wave action from the waters of Pleistocene Lake Lahontan. Core sampling conducted around Walker Lake in 1984 found evidence of rapid filling of the lake between 5,500 and 4,500 years ago (Benson, Meyers, and Spencer 1991). There is at least one Clovis site on the southern tip of Walker Lake (Tuohy 1985:table 1), indicating that people have lived in the area since at least 10,000 to 12,000 years ago.

A broad V has been cut through the terrace in front of Copper Canyon by water action, and numerous white granitic boulders and alluvium have been deposited in the alluvial fan, with the pictograph boulder being at the "hub" of this fan. Proceeding up Copper Canyon, the V cut narrows dramatically as solid rock is encountered (forming very steep canyon walls). Bradbury, Forester, and Thompson (1989:264) concluded that until around 4700 B.P. Walker Lake filled in successive phases that occurred rapidly. However, the filling phase that commenced around 2000 B.P. was more progressive and slow in character. Benson, Meyers, and Spencer (1991:206) conducted research that found evidence of flooding resulting from increased discharge from Walker River, though they were unable to conclude whether this was a single event or a series of floods.

Other evidence of flooding comes from changes in the channel of Walker River to its present course during the late Holocene. It is fairly well established that the original course of the Walker River was through Adrian Valley (Jones 1925:46; Russell 1885:279) and that major flooding in the Mason Valley was responsible for changes in channel (King 1978:37). Walker River's current and paleo channels share the same point of bifurcation in the area of maximum shoreline of Walker Lake. As these channels have almost equal gradients, frequent shifts in channel can be expected. For example, the lower Carson River in the Carson Desert changed its course many times during the Holocene (Morrison and Davis 1964:103), with major channel changes occurring even historically (Morrison and Davis 1964:105; Russell 1885:44–45). Sedimentation and erosion resulted in changes in the channel of the lower Carson during large floods, and it is likely that although the history of the Walker River is not as well known, changes in its river channel also occurred during major flooding in northern Mason Valley (King 1978:37).

We have argued that the Agai-Pah pictograph site may illustrate some of the themes regarding a great flood that are implicit in Walker River Paiute oral traditions of a sea serpent dwelling in the lake. Geological evidence suggests major flooding episodes in the past, and such episodes may have been recalled in oral traditions of the Walker Lake sea serpent. Whether or not the Agai-Pah pictographs were made to represent this tradition is not something that can be known from archaeology alone. In any case, rock art (like other forms of symbolism) is open to reinterpretation and incorporation in novel cultural contexts. If the Agai-Pah pictograph site is to have a cultural resonance in the present for Walker River Paiutes, it needs to be viewed from the perspective of local oral traditions.

CHAPTER 3

The Mountain Maidu Homeland

Native and Anthropological Interpretations of Cultural Identity

HELEN VALBORG AND FARRELL CUNNINGHAM

Maidu people of the northeastern Sierra Nevada (see figure 1.1) trace the creation of the world along a series of landmarks in Plumas and Lassen counties, California. They identify the Trail of Worldmaker as he moved along the rivers between Quincy and Susanville. Traditional anthropological investigations of the area suggest that the Mountain Maidu were relative latecomers to the territory. Archaeologists have assigned much of the rock art and other prehistoric site remains to pre-Penutian populations. These studies appear to contradict contemporary Mountain Maidu concepts of their origin and their relationship to the land. This chapter explores the seeming contradiction and compares Maidu and anthropological modes of interpreting the past with respect to issues of cultural identification with a homeland. It follows the form of a dialogue between the archaeological and ethnographic evidence and the Mountain Maidu identification with the land through myth, language, and an intimate knowledge of environmental systems and locales. This anthropological exploration is based upon several sources, including the important archaeological works of Makoto Kowta, who has devoted many years to the study of Maidu pre-history (Kowta 1969, 1988, 2000, 2001). The Mountain Maidu perspective is contributed by members of the Plumas County Maidu community and the Maidu Cultural and Development Group.

THE ARCHAEOLOGY OF MAIDU CULTURAL CHRONOLOGY

Before 3000 B.C. the archaeological record in the northeastern Sierra Nevada is relatively thin. Older projectile points found in the Plumas County area are the Northern Side-notched types, followed by the Pinto point type, both belonging to the Great Basin Archaic Tradition. The Pinto Complex has been associated with the westernmost distribution of big-horn sheep (Grant 1980). Its dispersal suggests that Great Basin hunters ventured sporadically into the high mountains of the area in search of bighorn sheep and other incidental game from as early as 6000 B.C. It also suggests that inhabitants of the Great Basin considered the eastern Sierra Nevada as part of their potential subsistence territory from early times.

To the west of the Sierran crest, the "Milling Stone Horizon" that had persisted for several thousand years in California stretched up the great inland valleys but had not yet penetrated into the central and northern Sierras (Kowta 1969; Wallace 1955; Warren 1968). Between 3000 and 2000 B.C. population increased as people representing the Milling Stone Hori-zon settled more intensively into all corners of the Central Valley. This intensification resulted in population growth that took place during a period of climate warming, and an expansion of oak that began to flourish at elevations 300 meters beyond previous altitudinal limits for oak. All this encouraged human movement up into the foothills. Several anthropolo-gists have associated this intensification with the ancient cultural substra-tum of Hokan-speaking people in California. They identify such foothill traditions as the Mesilla Culture at Oroville and possibly the Windmiller Complex along the Cosumnes and Mokolumne Rivers with a movement of Hokan people into the flanks of the northern Sierras (Kowta 1988:66; True et al. 1979).

Around 2500 B.C. a distinctive cultural tradition emerged in the Cen-tral and Northern Sierras and was named after the Martis Valley in Placer County. This archaeological culture has been traced from the Tahoe Basin to Hallelujah Junction and Bucks Lake in Plumas County (Elston 1971, 1979;

Riddell and Pritchard 1971). Kowta points out that the Martis Complex, as originally conceived by Heizer and Elsasser (1953), was "represented on both sides of the Sierran crest from south of Lake Tahoe northward to the south of Honey Lake, generally within the Transitional Life Zone between the elevations of 2500 feet to 6000 feet" (Kowta 1988:68). This tradition is characterized by basalt chipped stone tools, not unlike the large projectile points of the pre-Penutian Mesilla Complex or the Windmiller Complex, and a subsistence pattern that emphasized hunting over seed processing.

There is much debate about who the Martis people were. Olsen and Riddell (1963) argue that people of the Mesilla Culture occupied the western flanks of the Sierras while the Martis Tradition was to be found on the eastern side. Farber (1982) differentiates eastern and western Martis cultures, assigning the eastern to Hokan-speaking people and the western to Penutian-speaking people. Moratto, on the other hand, connects the Martis Tradition as a whole with Penutian speakers (1984). Elston (1971) believes that the Martis Tradition represents a Sierran exploitation by both California and Great Basin groups who possessed similar tool kits, while Kowta thinks the Martis Tradition was a mix of California and Great Basin, with California characteristics predominating. Kowta believes that these people were Hokan-speakers who were displaced up into the Sierras by intrusive Penutian groups who were moving into California from the north. He also believes that the Hokan-speaking Modoc were involved in the development of the Martis Tradition (Kowta 1988). All of these interpretations seek to establish a chronology that is based upon material culture typological evidence derived from archaeological residues. They produce a model of cultural identity as it moves through time and place.

THE MAIDU CONCEPT OF CULTURE IN TIME

In the world, time passes whether people exist or not. Without people, however, time exists without there being any knowledge of its existence and, because of this, time becomes meaningless. Though time exists and there is a passage of events, actions, energies forming and reforming, time ceases to exist as meaningful without individuals to enact its passage through their experience of action and energy. Though time may have passed, the individual person experiences, in each moment, the energies put down since time began through world construction within the mind. Individuals create the world and all of its interpretations through experience in time.

Sequences in anthropological chronology produce a fragmentation of Maidu cultural identity. This is because the cultural presence has been lifted out of a community of experience that possesses its own very different knowledge of time. Attempting to communicate a Maidu concept of time in a language and form that represent the cultural lens to which anthropology belongs seems to be almost an impossibility. Even so, it must be assumed that the Maidu are capable of fully considering and reflecting upon a shared human experience and must, therefore, be capable of integrating it into an identity that possesses its own continued world order.

Units of time in this world order are embedded in individual and group experience. Seasons, cycles of growth, lifetimes, procurement patterns are all measured in terms of human experience. Time is not divided into measurable units that attempt to transcend the individual or the group. The Maidu worldview might best be understood through measured units of experience. These experiences may be personal and immediate or may exist through reconstruction in the human mind. Altogether, these accumulated experiences result in a complete Maidu cultural identity.

ROCK ART EVIDENCE AND CULTURAL IDENTITY

Since the 1920s, archaeologists have attempted to differentiate styles of rock art and use them as a diagnostic means for establishing chronological sequences and cultural affiliations. Identifiable styles are based upon statistically measured occurrences of elements, trait clusters, and manufacturing techniques. In their work on the rock art of Nevada and eastern California, Heizer and Baumhoff utilized five style categories (Heizer and Baumhoff 1962:197). The rock art of Plumas and Lassen counties includes their Style 1 (cupules) and Style 2 (grooves and cupules), but also incorporates an additional Style 6 (Abstract Valley Sierran) and Style 7 (High Sierra Abstract Representational). Baumhoff thought Styles 1 and 2 were associated with an ancient Hokan culture in California (Baumhoff 1980). If he is correct, these styles (as they occur in other areas where Penutian-speaking people like the Maidu live) may be considered pre-Penutian. Style 6 occurs in areas that have been associated with the Miwok, who, like the Maidu, are Penutian speakers. Dixon believed that the Mountain Maidu may have used this style to mark the margins of their boundaries (1905:225). Payen argues that such boulder rock art may have been the sites of fertility ceremonies focused on the increase of plants and animals as well as humans (i.e., "fertility magic") (1966). He believes that the degree of repatination of Styles 6 and 7 in the area suggests an association with Martis materials. He also notes the strong similarities between Style 7 and that of Great Basin Representational and Abstract Curvilinear Styles (Payen 1966). Kowta hypothesizes that Style 1 represents early Hokan (including early Martis) and Style 2 late Hokan (late Martis). He also suggests that Style 7 represents an early Great Basin contribution to the Martis Tradition (1988). Despite the differences in these interpretations, there seems to be a general agreement among anthropologists that the rock art in Plumas and Lassen counties is pre-Maiduan and relates to Hokan-speaking people. It is important to note, however, that the Mountain Maidu ethnographic record indicates that they hunted bighorn sheep (Dixon 1905) using blinds that have been identified in Plumas and Sierra counties, particularly at Hawley Lake. It is possible, therefore, that the Hawley Lake petroglyph depicting a bighorn sheep identified by Payen as pre-Penutian is, in fact, the work of the Mountain Maidu (Payen and Scott 1982).

The Hawley Lake site is located at a high elevation (ca. 1980 meters) overlooking a game trail that follows a stream flowing below lofty peaks of high-grade basalt. The petroglyphs are engraved on a huge sloping surface of talc magnetite at the principal site, and on the same material at two lesser nearby sites. One hundred thirty-nine different elements are depicted in a prolific display of abstract curvilinear and angular figures, as well as anthropomorphs, animals, and animal tracks. Animal tracks make up 26 percent of the motifs at this site and are diagnostic of Style 7, the High Sierra Abstract Representational (Payen and Scott 1982). The varying degrees of repatination of the motifs suggest a long period of seasonal habitation extending from around 2000 B.C to the historic period. Though archaeological evidence at the site has been identified as Martis (Payen and Scott 1982), by the time research at the site was undertaken, a great deal of informal surface collection had occurred, resulting in the removal of more recent artifacts. Many of the petroglyphs show a close relationship to Great Basin Abstract Curvilinear and Representational styles, which suggests continued use of the site by Great Basin people coming up into the Sierras to hunt and, possibly, to quarry the high-grade basalt. Similarities with rock art styles on the western slopes of the Sierras suggest movement of people up the Yuba River. Though the use of the Hawley Lake site by the Mountain Maidu people is mentioned in the ethnographic record (Dixon 1905), it is difficult to ascertain which of the petroglyph elements are theirs. The clearly identifiable bighorn sheep figure and the ovine animal tracks correspond with early stories of Maidu hunting practices in the area, but these stories did not include descriptions of rock art production.

Other rock art sites in the area are located at lower elevations and occur in association with bedrock mortars, places of seed collection, and game trails. At the bedrock mortar sites petroglyph styles 1, 2, and 7 can be found on large boulders situated in open valleys, close to streams. Most of these boulders are glaciated granite, some of them, such as those at Bird Creek, pecked with elaborate designs over an area of 4.6 × 6 meters. There are few caves containing rock art in the area, though a shallow recess in Squaw Queen Valley contains red ochre smudges and the outline of a human hand. Archaeological investigations in this part of eastern Plumas County suggest prehistoric usage of the area by several different cultures, including Great Basin groups as well as Mountain Maidu and, possibly, Hokan-speaking Modoc from the north (Elston 1979). Artifacts dating to 8000 B.P. indicate very early usage of the area by Great Basin people (Daniel Elliot, personal communication 2002), who may have been responsible for some of the heavily repatinated rock art sites extending through Sierra Valley to the Gold Lakes Basin. Basalt lithic scatters exist at many of these sites, attesting to the importance of this material as a tool stone, and temporally diagnostic point types indicate its utilization over thousands of years, including the period attributed to Maidu habitation.

Though the archaeological evidence is not extensive, it is generally assumed by archaeologists that the Martis people continued to live in the Northern and Central Sierras for 3,000 years. There they hunted, fished, milled seeds, and eventually engaged in acorn processing. Around A.D. 500, however, they apparently responded to the increased aridity in climate by leaving the area and retreating to the eastern Tahoe Basin. This movement reduced human usage of the northern Sierras and created a hiatus that provided an opening for subsequent habitation. The evidence seems to suggest that after this period of very low human density, the Mountain Maidu began moving into the area around A.D. 1000. Kowta warns that it is difficult to separate Martis from Maidu deposits at the few sites that have been excavated in the Plumas and Lassen areas. Nevertheless, it can generally be stated that "evidence of a Maidu arrival in the area around A.D. 1000 [can be] signaled by the appearance of Gunther Stemmed and Desert Side-notched points and increased use of mortars" (1988:160). The increased use of mortars is especially interesting in light of the fact that Dixon (1905) recorded that the Maidu had a dread of mortars and would not touch them. They were believed to be used by shamans and were considered "abiding places of powerful spirits" associated by some with Coyote or Earthmaker [Worldmaker] (Dixon 1905:137). In light of this, some anthropologists have assumed that the mortars found in the area were manufactured by the Martis instead of the Maidu.

MAIDU VIEWS ABOUT ARTIFACTS AND ROCK ART

The Mountain Maidu interpretation of artifacts and rock art found in their homeland is fluidic, because the experience of interaction with any given artifact and any given rock art site is of an individual nature. Since, however, collective individual experiences create community cultural identity, some ideas do exist that might be considered to belong to the Mountain Maidu in general with regard to such things.

The Mountain Maidu regard artifacts as living. That is, they contain energy that is capable of transference from within the form to the external world. The energy is contained yet fluid, capable of influencing the world around itself. Artifacts contain the energy of the world creation. This energy may most adequately be described as songs. Perhaps one song might be the song of Worldmaker and Coyote sung at the beginning of the world, while another song might be the song that caused this energy to take its original form. The song may be one of infinite experience or it may be that of the human who created the artifact. These songs do not remain excluded from living human experience. It is necessary only to interact with an artifact to begin to hear its song, its balance of energy, and know the story of the artifact. Thus artifacts and rock art remain a part of the living human worldview and cultural identity.

The artifacts and rock art are real and their energies and songs continue to create and re-create the Maidu world. Within a cultural system that maintains fluidity of experience, artifacts and rock art cannot become the product of "others," nor can they be externalized from the Maidu world. To take these objects that are part of a complete Maidu cultural system and make of them abstract objects created by a remote and untouchable people is to cause the Maidu cultural system to become incomplete. In short, these objects contain living energy, affect individuals and the Maidu community as a whole, and are part of the Mountain Maidu world. They should not be separated or viewed as separate from human existence and experiential potential. Individuals may learn songs from the stones, they may learn from the spirit world, and they may have dreams and religious experiences as a result of interacting with artifacts or rock art. Even though these objects may be buried or unknown, they remain containers of Maidu identity and potential. An improperly handled artifact may even cause sickness or death to the living.

THE LINGUISTIC EVIDENCE

Paralleling the archaeological evidence, linguistic data suggest that Penutian-speaking peoples began moving from the north into California and penetrating its Central Valley around 1000 B.C. (Kowta 1988; Owen 1965). The fact that California Penutian speakers occupy a large area in the Central Valley and are surrounded by Hokan-speaking groups has inspired the idea that early and widespread Hokan-speakers were displaced by intrusive Penutian-speaking peoples (Baumhoff and Olmsted 1963; Kroeber 1955). It has been suggested that a series of successive Penutian entries into California occurred, contributing to the breakup and divergence of the ancient Hokan community (Whistler 1977). Shipley and Smith have suggested that the three branches of the Penutian-speaking Maiduan people—Nisenan, Konkow, and Mountain Maidu—represent three separate migrations into California. The basis for this scenario derives from their study of linguistic terms for plants and animals, including those borrowed from neighboring peoples. Shipley and Smith determined that the Valley Nisenan and the Foothill Konkow are more closely related to each other and that the Mountain Maidu are more divergent (Shipley and Smith 1979). Using a classic historical linguistic approach, Richard Levy's glottochronological reconstruction suggests that a proto-Nisenan and proto-Konkow split took place around A.D. 500, the Konkow moving up into the Feather River Canyon, leaving the Nisenan in the Sacramento Valley. He identifies a subsequent split between the Konkow Maidu and the Mountain Maidu that took place around A.D. 1000 and marks the movement of the Mountain Maidu into the higher elevations of the Plumas and Lassen counties area (Levy 1979). This linguistic evidence seems to support many of the archaeological interpretations, particularly those that associate the shift in populations into the high mountains with the displacement of Hokan-speaking peoples by invasive Penutian-speaking groups.

MAIDU LANGUAGE AND HOMELAND

From a Maidu perspective, their language came into being as the expression of experiences with infinite energies that formed into sound. In gathering layers of meaning and understanding, the sounds became capable of transcending individual expression and became the carrier and creator of collective human experience. During the time of creation known as *beteyto*, Worldmaker created many different types of people and languages. Maidu creation begins in an obscure place, a great place filled with something like fog where patterns for this world were informed. The energy begins to take form and the world as we know it begins to take shape through the thoughts of Worldmaker.

The world described in the unfolding Maidu creation story is one that correlates with the present-day Mountain Maidu homeland. The language describes familiar mountains, streams, and trees. The animal people who lived during the *beteyto* are the animals of the contemporary Maidu homeland. Finally, during *beteyto* Worldmaker actually creates the landscape, shapes it, forms it, causing the events that give it the characteristics that humans would know. These are the multiple landmarks where the events of Maidu genesis occurred. Rock formations, river pools, lakes, forests, and plant populations—all exist and are evident to the eye and all form the foundation of what is a Maidu cultural worldview. The Maidu believe that their language expresses the experience of this genesis, this formation of their homeland.

Words in the Maidu language such as *watkum* (mallard), *bubum cham* (pine tree), and *chuchuyam ba* (a rock formation commonly called Soda

Rock) are all words that demonstrate implicit as well as explicit meanings and understandings of the Maidu world. *Watkum* is a word imitative of the sound a mallard makes, *wat* being the sound while *kum*, added as a suffix, denotes the one who says *wat*. *Bubum cham*, as a word, carries an implicit understanding of the role of pines in the ecosystem, *bu* being derived from the Maidu word *buwom* (wind) and *bubum* carrying a connotation of lessened wind. The implicit ecosystem understanding is the idea that an oak-pine combination forest will allow for the pines to act as a windbreak, in order that acorns will not fall out of oak trees too early. *Chuchuyam ba* speaks of the mythological origins of the rock formation while also including a practical resource, salt. *Chuchuyam* literally means "urine" in English. Monster women once lived at this place, killing people with their urine until Worldmaker instigated their demise. *Ba*, translated into English, means "salt." There was, even in historic times, a unique species of grass growing at this locale that produced a type of salt when it was burned.

The above words might be taken as evidence that a fully developed speaking system was present when the Maidu first encountered these places and things. These words might also be taken as evidence that the language was formed by these places and things. The places and things of this land are the carriers of the energies involved in Worldmaker's creation. As they are named and expressed in language they are brought to life. The words and the various components of the land have the power to create and re-create the Maidu perspective each day in a lifetime and during every generation. This is the basis for the conviction that the Maidu people, as a people, were created here in this homeland and that the Maidu language, as a language, was created here as well.

AN ANTHROPOLOGICAL ANALYSIS OF MAIDU MYTHOLOGICAL TIME

In a paper on the historicity of Maidu Myths, Makoto Kowta examines the chronology of mythical motifs belonging to the three branches of the Maidu people by correlating them with anthropological data. Kowta identifies three mythic "ages" named after dominant Maidu mythical figures: the Age of Coyote and Wonomi, the Age of Onkoito, and the Age of Kodoyampe (Kowta 2000). Kowta relates the Age of Wonomi to a proto-Nisenan branching, which, according to archaeological and linguistic evidence, he places at A.D. 500. This was a time when the Maidu saw themselves as part of the natural world, not separate from it. Kowta refers to their reluctance in the mythology to kill and eat other creatures. This could relate to a time of generalized hunting and gathering. Kowta marks A.D. 800 as the beginning of the Age of Onkoito, which he relates to a proto-Konkow branching. This was a time of drought and difficulty, during which the Maidu had to use their wits and act upon nature. He believes that the celebration of human prowess was expressed in the anthropomorphic hero Onkoito, with whom the Maidu identify. Following this, the Age of Kodoyampe describes a time when the hero could not save the Maidu from death. Kowta correlates this period, beginning around A.D. 1400, with the plagues of Coyote and the coming of the white man. He relates the Mountain Maidu branching and movement into their Plumas and Lassen counties homeland with this last age.

According to Dixon's (1912) interpretation of Maidu mythology, the first sentient beings (First Man and First Woman) came from the north to settle in the southern part of the Maidu area (identified as the Marysville Buttes). By and by, people came to be. Coyote then introduces death and languages, and tribes diverge. Eventually Worldmaker tells Coyote that he is going off to the east, to Tsu'tsuyen [sic] or Soda Rock. There he subdues monsters and creates plants and animals in preparation for humans (1912). Kowta (2000) interprets this to mean that the proto-Nisenan came from the north and initially settled in the Central Valley area of California. There they experienced population growth, language divergence, and subsequent settlement expansion into the foothills and, finally, into the Mountain Maidu homeland in the northeastern Sierras. This interpretation works well with the linguistic and archaeological evidence presented here.

THE MOUNTAIN MAIDU INTERPRETATION
OF MYTH AND PLACE

All of the places within the Maidu world that are features recognizable from the creation stories are also places of resources. These places form, in part, the structure of the Maidu culture. Within the Maidu world numerous rocks, pools, hilltops, and lakes hold significance as places where the individual may go in order to gain knowledge. Such places, crisscrossing the Maidu homeland, are physical reminders of the world creation. Some of these landmarks, taken collectively, are known as Worldmaker's Trail—this was the route Worldmaker took in order to look over the land in preparation for the coming of the humans.

The landmarks and features mark the points along this route at which Worldmaker carried out some world-preparatory action. Each of these landmarks contains a story of its creation. Keddie Ridge, in central Plumas County, is known as Yakum Yamani (Canoe Mountain) in Maidu. For example, in Maidu mythology Worldmaker attempted several times to lead the people in eliminating Coyote from the scheme of things. During the last great attempt Worldmaker caused the world to be flooded. A canoe carrying the people came down upon the mountain as the flood subsided, and this peak came to be known to the Maidu as Yakum Yamani. Unfortunately, Coyote was in the canoe, and so after the flood he was still in this world. Thus, we have a world in which varied experience and energy are present. The mountain might serve as a daily reminder that personal responsibility is essential in this world. Humans must balance the creative harmony of Worldmaker with the divisive disruptions of Coyote in their daily lives. Other landmarks were created along the route where bear grass, which would be used in basket weaving, would flourish, salmon would spawn, and deer would come to drink. All of these places are indelibly registered in the language of the people and are acknowledged by them through ritual practices and procurement etiquette. Maidu people of the area do not consider it possible that this homeland, which resides at the heart of their language, their environmental knowledge, and their cultural identity, could have belonged to them for a mere few hundred years. They do not believe they could have constructed the whole tapestry of their cultural identity as it is embedded in the land in such a short length of time. Their view of time as measured units of experience enables them to tap into events and places of their occurrence that stretch back to the beginnings of creation.

In short, the Maidu are the people whose creation story begins here, in this area of the Sierra Nevada Range. This founding point of identity can never·be extricated from any form of identity possessed by Mountain Maidu individuals who, even without knowing all the details of the story, remember that their creation was in this land.

IS THERE A COMMON GROUND WHERE INTERPRETATIONS CAN MEET?

Anthropological interpretations empower individuals, giving them a broad understanding of the world through an examination of cause and effect as it is expressed in cultural adaptation and change. These interpretations focus on questions of cultural identity with time and place and form. They provide the investigator with an overview of evolving humanity, one that does not necessarily require a personal experience of the cultural expressions in question. Compared to this, the Maidu approach to understanding their own culture is vastly different. Not only does it depend upon a personal experience of cultural expressions, but it depends upon an ability to commune subjectively with the environment in a manner that animates things quite independently from sequential chronologies. The Maidu seek understanding in a world where knowledge is gained through understanding living energies that are contained within the landscape and that potentially transcend it. This is a world where a stone may sing and a tree can talk. It is a world where rock art has the potential to change someone's life or a simple artifact can provide a key to seeing into a new world. In such a world there is no cultural ownership of artifact or rock art. The energy that these objects and the land itself transmit extends beyond the categories that are meaningful in anthropology.

A common ground exists in the desire of both anthropologists and native peoples, such as the Maidu, to understand the world. In sharing this concern, it seems that anthropologists are being nudged to the perimeters of science by native peoples who persist in identifying their own cultures in their own ways. Relative perceptions of time and space have long been acknowledged in anthropology (Gellner 1985), but these have been treated as alternative "realities," which could be examined within the framework of a more absolute reality supported by scientific suppositions and methodologies. While this view may be justified within the discipline of anthropology, it may not enable anthropologists to penetrate the actual cultural experience of members of a native group that is in the process of experiencing its own cultural expression. In the contemporary world, a powerful assertion of indigenous cultural identity is taking place. It is a process whereby people become self-consciously aware of who they are in connection to time and place. This process and the validity of these reemerging identities need to be respected and understood on their own terms. Perhaps a willingness to consider that both the anthropological and the native worldviews regarding cultural identity can be treated as relative will provide the only means to find a common ground for understanding.

PART II   ROCK ART'S SOCIAL CONTEXTS PAST AND PRESENT

CHAPTER 4

Toward a Gender-Inclusive View of Rock Art in the Northern Great Basin

WILLIAM J. CANNON AND ALANAH WOODY

Androcentrism in the interpretation of the archaeological record has been recognized as a problem for many years (Conkey and Spector 1984; Gero and Conkey 1991; Leach 1999), and it is one that many researchers have tried to eliminate from their work. In at least one area of archaeological research in the Great Basin, however—the study of rock art—male bias seems to remain as strong as ever. In this chapter we argue that such a bias is just as inappropriate in rock art studies as it is in other areas of research. Specifically, we discuss both theoretical assumptions and methodological inconsistencies that contribute to the continuation of this bias in Great Basin rock art research. We examine rock art in the Northern Great Basin, then present data demonstrating that rock art is often found in direct association with habitation sites and ground stone (see also Cannon and Ricks [chapter 8], Pendegraft [chapter 5], and Shock [chapter 6], this volume), a pattern repeated elsewhere in the Great Basin (Green 1987).

A direct correlation between ground stone artifacts and the presence of women, especially from very early periods, of course cannot be assumed (McGuire and Hildebrandt 1994). It is important to note that we are emphatically not saying that all ground stones were the exclusive property of women; that was certainly not the case. There was, however, a sex-based division of labor among hunter-gatherers in the Great Basin, and because "food processing is a task that almost universally falls to females (e.g., cooking, seed grinding)" (Bettinger 1991:101), the presence at rock art sites of tools used for this purpose (i.e., ground stone), in addition to other settlement archaeology, suggests the presence of women and the performance of female tasks. Given this implication, it seems just as likely that these female tasks were related to the production and/or use of the rock art at these sites as any other practice occurring there. Despite this implication (that rock art may in fact be female oriented), archaeologists generally interpret Great Basin rock art to be the product of men and associated with male activities and themes, such as hunting (Heizer and Baumhoff 1962) or male shamanistic rituals (Whitley 1994a, 1998c). The role of women in the production and use of Great Basin rock art has been, and continues to be, rarely considered.

A growing number of researchers in the United States and other countries, however, are beginning to explore the production of rock art by women as a logical possibility. Green, a number of years ago, examined the ecological contexts of southern Nevada rock art sites and suggested that whenever rock art is found in association with habitation sites and evidence of domestic activities, women may well have been the authors of at least some of the glyphs (1987:189). Elsewhere, Bass has examined Pecos River–style pictographs in West Texas and suggests that both females and males may have been involved in the creation of rock art (1994:68). She stresses that "we may propose that rock art may be shamanistic but not male." In the Southwest, Young (1988) has emphasized the role of female activities in providing important metaphors to Puebloan cosmology. In California among members of the Uto-Aztecan language family, rock art was made and used by girls during their puberty rite (Du Bois 1908; Sparkman 1908; Strong 1929). This practice is also discussed by Monteleone (1993), who suggests that pictographs in the Eleana Range of southern Nevada may have been produced as a part of girls' puberty ritual. More recently Ritter and Hatoff (1998) comment on the analogs between scratched rock art motifs and historic and prehistoric basketry designs, which suggest to them the possibility that scratched rock art may have been made by women.

The androcentric bias of rock art research has been challenged in other parts of the world. In Australia, both Bullen (1991) and Smith (1991) confront the presumed exclusion of females from rock painting and other religious activities, and in South Africa, Solomon (1992) has explored the possible role of women in the production and use of rock art. Nevertheless, Great Basin rock art research often maintains a tacit acceptance of an intrinsic relationship between male activities and rock art, in spite of strong archaeological and ethnographic evidence to the contrary. For example, women may have their own distinct ritual practices, which are often denied or denigrated by men (Godelier 1986).

Recently, Hays-Gilpin (2004) has provided a descriptive summary of the spectrum of research exploring gender in rock art, but her focus, as with most of those whose work she discusses, remains on the images themselves, at the expense of site contexts. We believe, and will show in this chapter, how such reliance on imagery alone to elucidate meaning both misleads and limits an understanding of the complexity of symbolic systems. Rock art imagery is more likely to represent the "condensation" of many meanings (in Turner's 1967 sense), and those meanings are fluid and contingent, providing a locus for interpretative dispute (Quinlan 2000a:19). Rock art must be considered alongside the other activities occurring at a site in order to understand its functions and meanings, because site context is potentially an extension of site meaning (Bradley 2000; Quinlan and Woody 2001, 2003).

ANDROCENTRISM AND INTERPRETATION

The "males only" bias in rock art research is a particularly serious problem that restricts research and may limit a better understanding of the past functions of rock art. While rock art sites hold a wealth of cultural information, the subjective nature of the data (Schaafsma 1986:215) and the ongoing controversies associated with the direct dating of engraved images make rock art more difficult than other types of archaeological data to integrate into prehistoric models (Bednarik 2002). Perhaps because of these challenges, rock art research seems to be especially vulnerable to speculation, and, once advanced, these speculative ideas often continue unchallenged and become a perfect example of what Binford called "myth making" (1981). While theoretical diversity exists in other areas of archaeological research, Great Basin rock art research suffers from a lack of competing theoretical models. In keeping with Kuhn's (1962) characterization of scientific method, rock art theory has tended to see one paradigm dominate analysis and limit other avenues of research. If archaeologists and other researchers (especially those who are not specialists) discuss rock art at all, they usually refer to whatever theory is currently in vogue (Bahn 1998:ix), regardless of the rock art's context within an archaeological site or within the environment. Consequently, little thought or emphasis is given to the development of alternative models of explanation that may better fit the available archaeological evidence.

For many years hunting magic theory was considered to be the "right" interpretation for Great Basin rock art (Heizer and Baumhoff 1959, 1962; Nissen 1982, 1995). Heizer and Baumhoff argued that Great Basin rock art is found primarily on game trails and/or at hunting ambush locales. In their view, the purpose of the art was to help bring success in the hunt (Heizer and Baumhoff 1962:11). However, their site descriptions often noted features such as middens as well as artifacts such as ground stone, associated with the rock art. Such features and artifacts were interpreted as being related to hunting, even though ground stone and other domestic materials would be more indicative of habitation sites. This interpretation of rock art as related to hunting also implied that it was created and used exclusively by males.

More recently, the neuropsychological model (Blackburn 1977; Hedges 1976, 1987; Lewis-Williams and Dowson 1988), which explores the origin of rock art in trance states and shamanistic practices, has been applied to the Great Basin (Whitley 1994c, 1998c, 2000a). This model's most prominent North American proponent, David Whitley, has suggested that rock art in the Great Basin was manufactured primarily by male shamans as a part of their rituals. While this model is broader in focus than the hunting magic approach, it too is flawed by androcentrism, for it uncritically emphasizes a shamanistic interpretation of rock art and assumes that shamans were invariably male (Whitley 1994b:83–84, 1994c:21–24). As Whitley's critics have pointed out (Quinlan 2000b, 2001), this is an unsafe assumption— among historic Great Basin groups only the Kawaiisu restricted shamanism to men (Driver 1937:102), and to the west, in northern California, nearly every group had female shamans, while in some groups shamans were primarily women (Spier 1930:255).

Another important dimension that is often overlooked when considering the appropriateness of the hunting magic and shamanistic models for the rock art of the northern Great Basin is the time period during which the rock art was created. Much of the rock art of the northern Great Basin shows evidence of having been made during widely separated periods of time (Cannon and Ricks 1999; Woody 1997a). Hiatuses in production exist during the 8,000 or more years when rock art was being made in the area. Motifs, styles, methods of manufacture, and themes also changed over time. Early rock art does not look like more recent rock art, and it was made differently (for example, the Great Basin Carved Abstract style; see Cannon and Ricks [chapter 8]). In general, more recent rock art contains higher percentages of representational zoomorphic and anthropomorphic imagery, while earlier rock art tends to be predominantly abstract. Designs are often more densely "packed" and engravings much deeper than in more recent rock art (Ricks 1995; Ricks and Cannon 1993:94; Woody 1997a:54). In addition, this early rock art is completely repatinated and much of it reworked (the designs were re-carved later, removing the patina) after it had weathered for thousands of years. This reworking of the rock art may represent the resurrection of an earlier tradition or an appropriation of an existing landscape monument by new cultural groups moving into the area. The movement of new peoples with different cultural beliefs and practice into an area has often resulted in the incorporation or appropriation of an earlier group's monuments (Bradley 1998:17). For example, the Spanish in South America often knocked down native religious centers and constructed Catholic churches over them. Bettinger and Baumhoff (1982:494) have suggested that Great Basin scratched rock art was made by incoming Numic populations directly over earlier pre-Numic engravings in an attempt to cancel the power of those earlier images. While this may well be true in some areas, in the northern Great Basin scratched rock art appears to be more a kind of augmentation to earlier rock art than an attempt to obliterate it (Woody 1997a:60). But whether obliteration or augmentation was the goal of scratched rock art, it is entirely possible that it was the work of later cultural groups in response to the cultural materials of earlier peoples.

Without archaeological artifactual evidence, it is dangerous to assume or hypothesize that a single theory derived from ethnographic sources from areas external to the Great Basin can explain the creation of rock art in the Great Basin over such a long period of time (Monteleone 1998). Archaeologists have always known that oral tradition must be used with caution, as was restated recently by Echo-Hawk (2000). Furthermore, many modern aboriginal populations of the Great Basin believe that they have always occupied historic tribal lands, but the length of time that these groups have occupied the region is currently a point of archaeological debate (Madsen and Rhode 1994). Whether or not the ancestors of historic populations were the creators of the rock art in the Great Basin, we cannot assume that the beliefs of historic populations were the same as those of populations existing 8,000 years ago. It would seem unlikely, given the circa 8,000-year period (with its hiatuses in production, changes in motifs and styles, and so on) that a single cultural practice carried out by historic peoples could account for the creation of all rock art for the entire prehistoric period. Clearly, while ethnography is useful in formulating theories about the production of rock art, it must be supported by the archaeological evidence.

SETTLEMENT CONTEXT OF ROCK ART

Ethnographic and archaeological data suggest that when the rock art of the northern Great Basin is considered together with its archaeological contexts, the popular theories of shamanism and hunting magic are inadequate for understanding many sites. In the Warner Valley area (south-central Oregon), as well as farther to the north, stone rings are present at many rock art sites; these seem to be the remains of residential structures. There is no mention in the regional ethnographies of constructed shelters being used in vision quests (Kelly 1932; Spier 1930), although to the north some groups on the Columbia Plateau sometimes used isolated sweathouses for this purpose (Ray 1940:236). Stone rings in the northern Great Basin are therefore more likely related to houses or shelters rather than to the pursuit of shamanistic powers, particularly in light of the associated settlement debris indicating a full range of domestic activities at these sites (table 4.1). A small number of rock art sites (5.1 percent) contain rock cairns, a constructed feature sometimes associated with vision

TABLE 4.1 | Associated Materials at Rock Art Sites in the Warner Valley Area

ASSOCIATED MATERIALS	NUMBER OF SITES	PERCENTAGE OF TOTAL ($T = 196$)
Ground stone	113	57.65
Stone rings	55	28.06
Hunting blinds	12	6.12
Other structures	11	5.61
Rock cairns	10	5.10
Lithics and/or projectile points	130	66.33
Cultural plants in immediate area	124	63.27
Water in the immediate area	134	68.37
Quarries	4	2.04
House pits	10	5.10
Rock shelters or caves	24	12.24
Burials	3	1.53

($N = 196$)
(after Ricks 1995)

questing among northern groups such as the Klamath (Spier 1930:93). *If* constructed cairns in the past were associated with shamanistic practices, this suggests that shamanism was related to only a very small number of rock art sites in the northern Great Basin.

In any case, ethnographically in the northern Great Basin, shamanistic powers were less frequently sought at locations in the landscape believed to be especially powerful (such as caves, springs, pools, or certain mountaintops) (Kelly 1932:190; Park 1938:109; Spier 1930:94; Steward 1941:282). Rock art is not generally found in any of these locations of recognized power (Monteleone 1998). One cave near Fort Churchill (in the Carson Sink, northwestern Nevada) where power could be obtained is reported to have pictographs near the cave (Fowler 1992:177). Native consultants did not suggest that the doctors who went to the cave to seek power there had made the pictographs. but simply that they were considered to be a sign of the presence of power (Fowler 1992:177). Generally, few (if any) direct references appear in historic ethnographies of Great Basin groups of rock art being produced in the context of shamanistic practices (this has produced considerable debate; see Hedges 2001; Monteleone 1998; Quinlan 2000a, 2000b, 2001; Whitley 1998c, 2000b, 2003; Woody 2000a).

It is also difficult to argue that rock art sites are strictly related to hunting magic, although a variety of lithic materials are found at most rock art sites. Little evidence of hunting activity such as game drives, blinds, butchering areas, or impact-fractured projectile points can be found at most of the rock art sites in the northern Great Basin. Furthermore, in general imagery of animals is much rarer than abstract motifs, and images of the animals most commonly hunted, such as rabbits and marmots, are completely absent. In contrast, many rock art sites are located within environs that also feature important food plants and often contain evidence such as deep middens, ground stone, and house features, suggesting that they are habitation residues of various types of residential mobility (Cannon and Ricks [chapter 8], Pendegraft [chapter 5], and Shock [chapter 6], this volume). Logically, the presence of such features and material culture items minimally indicates that activities other than just hunting or shamanistic practices took place at most rock art sites in the northern Great Basin.

The hunting magic and shamanistic models are limiting and inadequate for explaining many of the rock art sites in the Great Basin. Archaeological data collected at many of these sites, as well as ethnographic information, simply do not support either theory. Many, if not most, of the activities indicated by the associated archaeological record at rock art sites seem to be related to women's activities.

METHODOLOGICAL BIASES IN ROCK ART RESEARCH

In addition to the theoretical biases outlined above, the methods by which archaeological materials have been and continue to be documented have perpetuated androcentric interpretations of Great Basin rock art. Previously, researchers who recorded archaeological sites evidenced a tendency to record projectile points (traditionally interpreted as male hunting implements) in great detail, while artifacts traditionally interpreted as indicating female behaviors—especially ground stone— were overlooked or casually recorded (Adams 1993:61; Beck and Jones 1997:182; Schneider 1993:12). Recording biases were partly the result of the difficulty of dating, collecting, and storing ground stone artifacts, as well as the presumed chronological importance of diagnostic projectile points. Time available for fieldwork has also been a factor in what was recorded. One researcher working in the Bureau of Land Management Lakeview, Oregon, District, simply stated to one of the authors (Cannon) that ground stone was present at sites, but there was not enough time to record it all. This researcher did, however, take the time to plot the precise location of every projectile point.

Similarly, rock art often has not been recorded at archaeological sites. In one case of a site with stone house rings and other residential indicators, the report (on file at the Bureau of Land Management, Lakeview, Oregon District) includes photographs showing a rock art panel within one meter of an excavation unit, but no mention of this panel is made in the body of the report or in the captions of the photographs.

A reexamination of recorded sites in the Bureau of Land Management Lakeview, Oregon, District, revealed that many sites recorded as lithic scatters with projectile points also contain ground stone and rock art. In some cases rock art was recorded as a separate site even though it shared the same location as the lithic scatter. Because of the emphasis placed on artifacts that can be identified to type, such as diagnostic projectile points, other artifacts such as ground stone and rock art slipped in importance during the limited time available for recording site data. However, treating rock art as a separate monument class divorces it from the portable artifact classes with which it co-occurs, thereby constructing it as an archaeological feature beyond the purview of mainstream archaeology.

ALTERNATIVE APPROACHES: A CASE EXAMPLE FROM SOUTHERN OREGON

Many Great Basin rock art sites contain evidence of residential behaviors, such as house pits and stone house rings, as well as ground stone and midden deposits. The Lake County region of southern Oregon has many such sites, and although occupational materials are difficult to temporally correlate with the rock art, their spatial proximity simply suggests that alternatives to the androcentric interpretation of rock art as hunting magic or shamanism might be appropriate.

Data from rock art surveys conducted by Cannon and Ricks (1986; Ricks 1995; Ricks and Cannon 1993) and Woody (1997b) in the Warner Valley vicinity, Lake County, Oregon (see figure 1.1), are used here to explore the presence of females at rock art sites in the region.

The Tired Dam site, located in the uplands above Warner Valley, Oregon, is a good example of a multifunctional site where a wide variety of activities are represented in the archaeological record (Woody 1997b). Recorded features include rock art, stone house rings, and rock rings that may have been hunting blinds. House rings were identified as structures containing ground stone, faunal debris, fire hearths, or other types of artifacts such as beads. A large quantity of ground stone and chipped stone artifacts was recorded in association with these features. Hunting blinds are small enclosures above game trails. The area in front of these enclosures contains impact fracture projectile points, lithic debris, and cores or chopping-type artifacts that may have been used in butchering. Both female and male activities are associated with the production and use of the rock art at the site. The rock art is, in fact, more closely associated with the areas of ground stone and habitation features than with the possible hunting blinds, suggesting a closer relationship with female labor and symbolic themes.

The Long Lake area (Ricks and Cannon 1993; see also Cannon and Ricks [chapter 8], this volume), like the Tired Dam site, is a rock art site located in the uplands near Warner Valley; rock art, occupation features, and middens are found along 4 kilometers of a low basalt rim. The area is located within one of the largest stands of biscuit-root—an important food resource for northern Great Basin peoples (Couture, Ricks, and Housley 1986)—in the region. In addition, bitterroot, chokecherry, yampa, and other important food plants are found in the area. Along the Long Lake rim, directly associated with the rock art, are large numbers of bedrock milling stones and other ground stone tools, some uncovered during limited excavation (3 cubic meters) at the site (Cannon 1987) (figure 4.1). Northern Paiute consultants from the area reported that ground stone artifacts were often turned upside down and cached onsite (Kelly 1932:139), and three of the four milling stones recovered during excavation were found upside down.

Rock art at this site dates back at least 6,800 years (Cannon and Ricks 1986:12). Ricks's (1995) research at Long Lake suggests that the most likely tasks performed at this locale relate to plant gathering and processing, work that is traditionally associated with women (Bettinger 1991:101). The location, size, quantity, and relationship to residential features of the ground stone at Long Lake and similar sites in the Warner Valley area suggest that ground stone artifacts and features probably had domestic uses rather than ceremonial ones. Several of the large boulders at the Long

Figure 4.1. Milling stones recovered from excavations at the Long Lake site, Oregon. Photograph by W. J. Cannon

Lake site, as well as others in the area, have multiple large metate surfaces on them—as many as eleven on a single boulder. Barrett, describing the Washoe to the south, reports that women would gather at communal grinding locations to process food, mixing social interaction with economic tasks. Similar gatherings could account for the multiple surfaces at the Warner Valley area sites (1917:15). Some of the milling stone surfaces at Long Lake have been completely repatinated and are located in areas with similarly repatinated rock art (figure 4.2), which would tend to indicate that both the production of rock art and the processing of plants were long-lived practices at this and other sites in the area, extending back several thousand years or more. While hunting would probably have also taken place in the area, that does not appear to have been the major focus of native peoples' activities here. Instead, intensive use of uplands for long periods by family groups collecting root resources is more likely (Ricks 1995:131).

Lowland rock art sites, such as the Narrows site, are also often associated with habitation locations. These large sites often contain house pits and stone house rings, as well as deep midden deposits and often vast quantities of ground stone. Again, in this situation women as well as men

Figure 4.2. Bedrock milling stone and rock art in direct association, Long Lake, Oregon. Photograph by W. J. Cannon

are likely to have been present. It is unlikely that any hunting would have taken place directly at the site; however, on-site plant processing is strongly suggested by the artifacts. In many cases, bedrock mortars and milling stones are located on the same boulder as the rock art (see also Pendegraft [chapter 5], this volume).

In general, rock art sites in the Warner Valley area contain ground stone artifacts and chipped stone artifacts, as well as other evidence of habitation (see table 4.1). Only a small percentage of sites have lithics with no ground stone or other features present. Furthermore, ethnographic data for the area indicate that chipped stone tools were used not only in hunting but also for plant collecting and processing (Kelly 1932). Therefore, it cannot be automatically assumed that sites that contain only lithics (including projectile points and bifaces) are hunting sites or sites where male activities such as point production or reworking took place. Only 6 percent of rock art is directly associated with hunting blinds (see table 4.1); none was found to be associated with places that were traditionally believed by the Northern Paiute to be sites of supernatural power where visions could be sought. However, as noted above, 5.1 percent of rock art sites are associated with rock cairns, which may have been constructed as a part of ritual.

Therefore, in this area of the northern Great Basin rock art sites seem to be most heavily concentrated in upland environments, where major root resources are located. Rock art is frequently present at long-term residential sites used by the entire family, as evidenced by house structures, midden deposits, and a full range of artifact types. If rock art was produced and used in male shamanistic or hunting rituals, one wonders whether the family living area would have been a likely place to conduct these rituals. Ethnographic accounts for the Northern Paiute who occupied this area historically suggest no type of hunting rituals at all and indicate that vision quests were not typically conducted in or near residential sites. Instead, sacred mountains, springs, and caves were the most common sites of such activities. Usually these powerful places were located at some distance from settlements (Kelly 1932; Whiting 1950). It might take several days to visit one of these distant places and return to the occupation site. If it was important to create a graphic record of one's vision imagery immediately after the vision experience so that memory of it would not be lost (as suggested by Whitley 1994c:4–5), the distance between sacred and residential locations would make that difficult. Consequently, most of the rock art of this area does not seem to fit the archaeological characteristics theorized by either the shamanistic or the hunting magic approach.

The central focus of this chapter has been to deconstruct the notion that women can a priori be ruled out of consideration as the makers of rock art. Many rock art sites occur in direct association with residential features (see table 4.1) and in areas of abundant plant resources. In general, plant harvesting and processing were the work of women (Bettinger 1991:101), and current research in the northern Great Basin and elsewhere reveals many rock art sites that do not fit the hunting magic or shamanistic models (see Pendegraft [chapter 5] and Shock [chapter 6], this volume). This research indicates that women and children certainly were present at rock art sites, and in some cases "women's work" appears to have been the dominant use of the locality. One is left to wonder if women are simply rejected from consideration as rock art makers because of the creativity involved, or "as soon as innovation or invention enters the picture" (Watson and Kennedy 1991:264).

Historically many researchers have treated rock art as if it were a separate phenomenon, not connected with other site materials and features (see Pendegraft, chapter 5). This position no doubt results from the difficulty of demonstrating temporal association, but rock art needs to be examined in context rather than separately from the rest of the archaeological materials of a site. While hunting or other primarily male or shamanistic activities certainly might have co-occurred at these rock art sites, archaeological evidence indicates that these activities are not the only plausible explanation for the rock art.

The two male-oriented theories—shamanism and hunting magic—that dominate the thinking of many archaeologists have been productive in stimulating debate. But now, with the inevitable accumulation of knowledge, the archaeological record itself dictates the need for a broadening of perspective and the development of new models to explain the functions and production of rock art. While the question of who produced the rock art is the focus of this chapter, many interesting questions about the production and use of rock art remain unanswered. For example, why does rock art seem to be concentrated in specific areas rather than spread more evenly across the landscape? Are there differences in the motifs that occur in different environmental contexts? Do rock art motifs change through time and if so, in what way? If the rock art is related to hunting, why are animals such as rabbits, deer, and marmots seldom represented in spite of being the most commonly hunted species? If the rock art is related to plant gathering, why do we not see plant imagery? These and other general research questions should be pursued without preconceived ideas about the gender of the art's makers and users.

Given the present state of the rock art record, such questions cannot currently be answered. But they never will be answered if interpretative models continue to extract rock art for analysis from its archaeological contexts. We believe it is those contexts that may inform the significance of the imagery. Furthermore, to continue to ignore the contexts of rock art use and production and to assume that rock art is androcentric (whether hunting or shamanism) create too narrow of a focus on a very small part of a multidimensional topic and inhibit the exploration of other important research questions. Rock art research in the Great Basin must follow the lead of researchers in other regions and attempt to eliminate both methodological and theoretical biases so that we may develop a more richly textured understanding of the lives of the people who experienced prehistoric rock art of the Great Basin in their daily routines.

CHAPTER 5

Grinding Stone and Pecking Rock

Rock Art of the High Basins, Spanish Springs, Nevada

SIGNA W. PENDEGRAFT

Though western North American rock art has been a subject of sporadic archaeological interest since the nineteenth century (Mallery 1893),
research has resulted in only vague understandings of the properties of
the imagery represented and its associated site contexts. For example, in
Nevada approximately 1,000 rock art sites have an official state record,
but only 244 of these actually record the presence or absence of associated cultural materials (Woody 2000a:138–43). Most site records contain
merely the word *petroglyph* or *pictograph* as a complete site description,
or else note the presence of easily identifiable motif categories such as
anthropomorphs or zoomorphs, ignoring the difficult-to-classify and for-
mally variable abstract imagery that characterizes the Basin and Range
Tradition (Woody 2000a:102, 184). Archaeological meanings are derived
from a consideration of context (Hodder 1986), making rock art interpretations that are based on inaccurate or incomplete characterizations of site
properties potentially flawed. Further, rock art theory, perhaps because of
the opaque character of its subject, has played a determining role in con-

structions of site properties, rather than data and theory being locked in a reflexive relationship. This is apparent from the problems associated with the two most popular theories of rock art functions applied to the Great Basin (hunting magic and shamanism).

In this chapter I discuss how the abundant site archaeology associated with rock art in the High Basins area of northwestern Nevada (see figure 1.1) cannot be satisfactorily interpreted from the perspective of the two most popular rock art theories used in western North America. My research underscores the need for careful and thorough documentation of site properties and illustrates that ignoring the domestic debris associated with rock art results in impoverished or misleading interpretation. In particular, the role of women in making and using rock art is often marginalized by distancing rock art from its settlement context, either by temporal distanciation or by overlooking residential debris. Both milling equipment and rock art itself are increasingly recognized as types of archaeology that are often underreported or simply overlooked (Adams 1993:61; Beck and Jones 1997:182; Schneider 1993:12; Cannon and Woody [chapter 4], this volume). As a result, women are written out of prehistory or relegated to reproductive tasks (economic and sexual), leaving "cultural" fields of society an exclusively male domain.

HUNTING MAGIC AND SHAMANISM IN NEVADA'S ROCK ART

Although landmark studies by Mallery (1893) and Steward (1929) represent the first major attempts to characterize the properties of rock art in the Desert West, it was not until the work of Heizer and Baumhoff (1962) that interpretation came to the fore in a synthetic study that reported sites from Nevada and eastern California sites. The theoretical importance of their work to Great Basin rock art studies is hard to overstate, for they introduced hunting magic to the region in a systematic way and sought to support it by reference to actual site characteristics (Quinlan and Woody 2001:213).

Heizer and Baumhoff explored the relationships between rock art and subsistence activities, regarding food procurement as the most important and time–consuming requirement for the survival of Great Basin peoples (1962:8) (strangely neglecting that securing food is the primary source of survival for all humans!). Their study of rock art site contexts concluded that there was a strong relationship between rock art and hunting activities, as rock art seemed predominantly located on animal migratory routes, in association with stone circles interpreted as hunting blinds, or at ambush venues at watering sources (Heizer and Baumhoff 1962:13–71). Drawing on ethnography, they noted that in certain cultural contexts male hunting shamans sought to ensure success in the hunt by enlisting the aid of supernatural agencies, and they theorized that this constituted rock art's aboriginal cultural context (Heizer and Baumhoff 1962:13, 15).

Establishing site contexts of rock art locales plays an important role in determining the art's potential audiences and the kinds of social routines in which it was embedded (Bradley 2000). Heizer and Baumhoff's hunting magic interpretation constructs rock art's distribution as distinct from domestic routines, distancing its use and production from activity areas representative of households. Their approach views Great Basin rock art as specialized in its distribution (the preserve of male hunters) and divorced from domestic routines that included women and children. However, such a construction discounts the presence of settlement debris, such as milling equipment and house rings, at a large number of Great Basin rock art sites, including the High Basins sites described below. Subsequent researchers have frequently noted the presence of domestic archaeology in direct association with rock art (Cannon and Ricks 1986; Quinlan and Woody 2003:374–75; Ricks 1995; Ricks and Cannon 1993), even at sites that formed the basis of Heizer and Baumhoff's approach (Quinlan and Woody 2001). It has become clear, as the research from the High Basins that I present indicates, that a full range of domestic activities seems to have been performed at many rock art locales; this evidence alters and adds to our perceptions of who interacted with the rock art and the kinds of social roles it may have fulfilled.

Heizer and Baumhoff are not unique in allowing theory to color their understanding of rock art site properties. For example, Cook and Fulmer's (1981) cultural resource inventory of the McCain Valley (eastern San Diego County, California) reports rock art sites associated with milling equipment, suggesting the presence of plant processing. Yet Cook and Fulmer emphasized male shamans as the creators of rock art (for ritual and sacred purposes), ignoring the associated archaeology that suggests multiple contexts of use and makers (in particular the presence of women and children) (1981:171–74). Such an interpretation repeats the standard archaeological trope of attributing apparently nonutilitarian or opaque site features a ritual function and also assumes that ritual specialists are predominantly male, in deference to an androcentric recording tradition predominant in the authors' archaeological heritage (Cannon and Woody [chapter 4], this volume).

Currently popular shamanistic approaches to Great Basin rock art also have a tendency to discount the archaeological context of rock art sites (Whitley 1994a, 1998c, 2000a). This approach argues that the actual character of rock art imagery can be used to determine its original cultural contexts, since rock art that encodes trance signifiers refers to trance states and thus shamanism (Lewis-Williams and Dowson 1988). Shamanism can be defined as the contact of spirits through trance for use as guardians and helpers of individuals (Layton 2000b:169) and is usually presented as a predominantly hunter-gatherer religious form (Ouzman 1998), though this view is not necessarily accurate (Lewis 1986, 1989). Consequently, the shamanistic or neuropsychological model theorizes that shamans record significant visionary experiences in rock art, explaining how it contains visual metaphors of trance states by incorporating entoptic phenomena in the motifs portrayed (Lewis-Williams and Dowson 1988). Rock art locales are viewed as the property of individual shamans functioning as vision-quest locales and, at least in the Great Basin, are usually spatially distinct from normal settlement archaeology (Whitley 1998a:22).

Considerable debate has taken place regarding whether it is really possible to use rock imagery by itself to resolve its cultural uses (Bahn 1988; Davis 1988; Dronfield 1996; Layton 1988, 2000b). By potentially focusing research on analysis of motifs present at rock art locales, researchers may succumb to a tendency to ignore the significance of rock art's associated archaeology as an additional source of meaning. Further, in some cases the associated archaeology is ignored or misunderstood, thus repeating Heizer and Baumhoff's (1962) debatable observation that rock art and settlement are only weakly associated in the Great Basin (Whitley 1998a:22)

The shamanistic approach also offers a lens through which to explore ethnography as a source of direct information regarding rock art's cultural contexts. A metaphoric approach to ethnographic data provides one way of teasing rock art information from otherwise opaque consultant commentaries

(Lewis-Williams 1981), though whether such information should be seen as more than establishing precedents for sources of hypotheses (Lewis-Williams 1991) is a legitimate point of debate (Quinlan and Woody 2003:374).

In the case of the Great Basin, it has been strongly argued that consultants cryptically expressed rock art's shamanic context to early ethnographers and only a metaphoric reading of the relevant ethnographic texts restores the consultants' intended reading of their commentaries (Whitley 1994c, 1998c). It is argued that shamans (predominantly, if not exclusively, male) made Great Basin rock art to record their visionary experiences, with rock art sites functioning as vision-quest locales where powers could be acquired (Whitley 1994c, 1998c). Actually, as critics of this general approach have pointed out (Quinlan 2000b), singing stands out in ethnographic accounts about shamanic activity, because the acquisition and ownership of songs were important sources of knowledge and power and were brought by spirits in dreams (Laird 1974; Park 1934). Here it is interesting to note that throughout the Great Basin (with the exception of the Kawaiisu), shamanism was not an exclusively male pursuit (though in some cases men may have predominated) (Park 1938). Yet, while alluding to this substantive criticism in a direct reply to a critical review (Quinlan 2000b:102), Whitley failed to respond, although it is a point that could be resolved clearly and unmetaphorically (2000b:108).

Critical examinations of such a use of the direct historical approach to Great Basin rock art (Hedges 2001; Monteleone 1998; Quinlan 2000b, 2001; Woody 2000a) highlight that these data are capable of sustaining various interpretations. Thus ethnography provides "an important source of inspiration for a wide range of divergent theories regarding rock art functions and symbolism" with multiple readings always possible (Quinlan and Woody 2003:374), particularly when dealing with cultural symbolism (Sperber 1975). Indeed, Whitley's understanding of the interpretive role of Great Basin ethnography has seen a significant evolution. In his early work (1982, 1987), Whitley argued that the absence of specific analogs meant that ethnography should be used broadly as a source of hypotheses—which is pretty much the position that he currently berates (Whitley 2000c, 2003; compare with Keyser and Whitley 2006).

Problems arise, therefore, not from the models themselves (both hunting magic and shamanistic) but from their over-application in rock art studies (Layton 2000b:179; Quinlan 2000b:102; Rector 1985:131), which spills over into popular perceptions (Quinlan [chapter 10], this volume) and into normative use, even in professional publications. This overuse of these two models calls the viability of the models themselves into question even when they do have legitimate and broad contextual application (Hedges 2001:134) or, at the very least, are theoretically plausible (Quinlan and Woody 2001:213). Further criticism concerns the way in which these two popular models have inhibited the exploration of alternative interpretations of Great Basin rock art, which either receive little attention or are aggressively argued against (Kehoe 2002; Monteleone and Woody 1999; Quinlan 2000b:96). Multiple working hypotheses should always be pursued, lest a single model becomes a ruling theory (Monteleone and Woody 1999:65). This broad approach is particularly important in rock art studies because arts (non-Western and Western) serve multiple functions and are highly social (Anderson 1979; Layton 1985; Layton 1991).

The effect of the popularity of hunting magic and shamanistic interpretations has been to establish as a "fact" that Great Basin rock art has no associated archaeology and was made and used almost exclusively by male ritual specialists (see also Cannon and Ricks [chapter 8] and Cannon and Woody [chapter 4], this volume). Even when an association between settlement activity and rock art is identified, the two are assigned to distinct temporal phases (Delacorte 1997; Whitley 1998b:3). This temporal dissociation is based more on an a priori assumption that domestic and ritual behaviors are spatially separate than on chronologies of rock art and settlement archaeology. It also does not adequately consider the possibility of contemporaneous use of rock art and settlement, forgetting that rock art's use-life is not limited to the act of its production. Monuments are re-used and incorporated into new cultural traditions (Bradley 1993:113, 1998:17), making it economical to assume that rock art, when encountered, would have provoked some kind of cultural response from subsequent cultural groups (Quinlan and Woody 2003:376).

ROCK ART IN CONTEXT: THE HIGH BASINS OF THE DRY LAKES PLATEAU, PAH RAH RANGE

Renewed interest in landscape theory in archaeology (Bender 1989; Bradley 1997, 2000; Tilley 1991, 1994; Ucko and Layton 1999) has led to rock art research's attaching greater significance to associated archaeological materials in understanding the art (Hartley 1992; Cannon and Ricks [chapter 8] and Cannon and Woody [chapter 4], this volume). This interest in landscape theory is one of the influences in the author's research in the High Basins area, northwestern Nevada, which explores the interrelationships between the various residues of settlement archaeology and rock art. The High Basins area of Spanish Springs Valley is located on the Dry Lakes Plateau of the southwestern portion of the Pah Rah Range. Numerous archaeological surveys of the area's rock art and settlement archaeology have been made over the past thirty years (Delacorte 1997; Johnson 1981; McLane 1980, 1999; Rusco 1969a, 1969b), but no full synthesis undertaken. Historically the area lies within the territory of the Tasiget-Tiviwari group of the Northern Paiute (Stewart 1941:362 and map 1). These historic inhabitants were known as the "between dwellers," perhaps because the southwestern boundary of their territory bordered that of the Washoe (Stewart 1941, 1966); little further ethnographic detail has been recorded.

The topography of the area surrounding the basins is characterized by basalt knolls on ridges, separated by saddles, rock outcrops, and talus slopes. The area ranges in elevation from 1,414 meters to 1,646 meters. Temperatures average 1 degree Celsius in January and 20.5 degrees Celsius in July. Precipitation has ranged from 3.5 to 34.2 centimeters per year since 1890 (Rusco 1981:1), and very occasionally the basins contain standing water (Alvin McLane, personal communication, 2002).

Modern vegetation is characterized by big sage (*Artemesia tridentata*), rabbit brush (*Chrysothamnus nauseous*), tumbling mustard (*Sisymbrium altissimum*), and invasive cheatgrass. Some present plants identified as possible food resources are Hookers balsamroot (*Balsamorrhiza hookeri*), wild onion (*Allium* sp.), Indian ricegrass (*Oryzopsis hymenoides*), Indian tea (*Ephedra viridis*), yampah (*Perideridia gairdneri*), biscuit-root and desert parsley (*Lomatium* sp.), and tansy mustard (*Descurainia pinnata*), to name a few. Local fauna include birds, antelopes, mule deer, badgers, jackrabbits, other small mammals, and reptiles.

Archaeological investigations were carried out in 1968 and 1969–70 by AmArcs of Nevada and the Nevada Archaeological Survey (Rusco 1969a, 1969b); four sites were excavated and eight others surveyed. In 1981 a cultural resource survey conducted for the City of Reno identified sixteen

SITE NUMBER	ROCK STRUCTURE	MILLING EQUIPMENT	PROJECTILE POINTS AND FORMAL CHIPPED STONE TOOLS	DEBITAGE
26wa1604	+	+	+	+
26wa1607	+	+	-	+
26wa1608	+	+	+	+
26wa1609	+	+	+	+
26wa1610	+	-	-	+
26wa1611	+	+	+	-
26wa1612	+	+	+	+
26wa1613	+	+	+	+
26wa1614	-	-	-	-
26wa2847	+	+	+	+
26wa2848	+	+	-	+
26wa2850	+	+	+	+
26wa2852	-	-	-	-
26wa2859	+	-	-	-
26wa5609	-	+	-	+
26wa5610	+	+	+	+
26wa5611	+	+	+	+
Totals	14	13	10	13

(Delacorte 1997; Johnson 1981; McLane 1999; Rusco 169a, 1969, 1981)

new sites (Johnson 1981). Alvin McLane has also compiled records for the rock art sites in the High Basins for the last few decades, detailed in a descriptive inventory report tallying more than 115 rock art sites (McLane 1999). And finally, Delacorte reports the results of an archaeological inventory undertaken in the area as part of the Tuscarora Gas Transmission Pipeline, which encountered a number of rock art sites in the area (Delacorte 1997). These sources provide the basis for my exploration into the interrelationships between rock art and settlement archaeology in the High Basins.

Table 5.1 details the relationship between rock art and settlement archaeology in this area. As can be seen, milling equipment is abundant, and rock rings occur in association with both rock art and milling equipment (figure 5.1). Some milling equipment exhibits a direct association with rock art, such as petroglyphs engraved on the milling stone itself (Alvin McLane, personal communication, 2002). Bedrock grinding slicks and petroglyphs sometimes co-occur on the same boulder surface and occasionally even overlap.

Figure 5.1. Rock art, rock rings, and ground stone at the Crow's Nest, High Basins, Nevada. Photograph by S. W. Pendegraft

Delacorte (1997:13) has built a localized chronology for the area, which has been used in this research. His chronology is based on dates from obsidian hydration analyses and radiocarbon assays, in addition to traditional temporally diagnostic projectile types. This evidence suggests that use of the High Basins area includes some Early Archaic occupation (7000–3500 B.P.), more Middle Archaic (ca. 3500–1300 B.P.) to mostly Late Archaic (1350–600 B.P.) settlement, and on up to historic times.

Interpreting High Basins Rock Art

Early research in High Basins rock art (Rusco 1969b) sought to test Heizer and Baumhoff's (1962) hunting magic theory by establishing whether the rock art was indeed associated with hunting features. Circular rock enclosures, similar to others interpreted by Heizer and Baumhoff (1962) as hunting blinds, most with rock art in association, were excavated by Rusco (1969b). These excavations found that the rock circles were "camp sites" or "habitation sites" (Rusco 1969b, 1981), rather than hunting blinds. Delacorte (1997:25, 32, 44) also reported archaeological contexts as supporting a residential interpretation of rock rings in the area. Yet recognition of the residential associations of High Basins rock art did not prevent a hunting magic interpretation being offered (Delacorte 1997; Johnson 1981), in contrast to Rusco's conclusions (Rusco 1969a, 1981, personal communication 2002).

Delacorte's (1997) informative archaeological survey of the Pah Rah Uplands reports rock art and settlement archaeology (milling equipment, rock rings, and so on) found in direct association in the High Basins/Dry Lakes Plateau area of Spanish Springs, northwestern Nevada (figure 5.2). Plant processing as well as hunting activities is suggested by these archaeological residues, implying that the rock art was located in or near campsites occupied by family units. Nonetheless, the petroglyphs are interpreted as falling into the magico-religious realm and having being created for the purpose of hunting magic (Delacorte 1997:27, 76, 145). When evidence suggested that rock art and milling slicks were of comparable age at one site, Delacorte (1997:27) commented, "This suggests the rock art and milling slicks may be of comparable antiquity, although the juxtaposition of supposedly magico-religious and domestic activities is surprising" (1997:27). The rock art was therefore attributed to the Middle and early Late Archaic, when "large vertebrate hunting intensified" (1997:27).

Figure 5.2. Rock art incorporated in a large rock ring, High Basins, Nevada. Photograph by S. W. Pendegraft

Delacorte's interpretation was partly based on the assumption that rock art that functions as a form of hunting magic reflects the importance of hunting in the economy of the culture that made it. Delacorte emphasizes High Basins rock art that portrays large game animals, the "frequent rendition" of bighorn sheep, indicating its basis in hunting magic (1997:77, 145). The settlement archaeology is dated by later diagnostic projectile points (Desert Side–notched and Rose Spring types) to a late prehistoric context (1997:76). Accordingly, Delacorte concludes that the bulk of the rock art predates the house structures because of the lack of evidence of intensive plant processing in earlier occupations. Delacorte does note that some continuation of rock art production into late prehistoric times is indicated by rock art panels depicting anthropomorphs with bow and arrow (1997:28, 29).

Delacorte's temporal separation of rock art from settlement archaeology is predicated on his assumptions that hunting magic would largely have been practiced only when hunting was the primary economic focus and that the imagery of the rock art is predominantly related to hunting themes. My own motif analysis, however, based on eleven sites from the High Basins area, suggests that direct representations of hunting themes are neither the dominant nor even a common motif type (Pendegraft 2005). Further, if Delacorte is correct to assign the production of much High Basins rock art to a period predating settlement archaeology, does this mean that later cultural groups using the area were oblivious to it, even though its juxtaposition (figure 5.3) to the settlement archaeology means it would have been part of the lived experience of daily life?

Certainly, hunting magic could have occurred in or near areas of residential activity (Quinlan and Woody 2001), and High Basins petroglyphs often occur on the outcrop walls abutting rock rings, as well as in association with domestic debris. Rock art's association with settlement archaeology would suggest that any hunting magic rituals took place with nonhunters also present. Site context can help determine whether rock art would have been encountered in the course of normal domestic routines or whether its location restricted access to it (Bradley 2000; Quinlan and Woody 2003:374). The High Basins rock art is situated in the midst of domestic routines and would have been encountered by both sexes, and this fact needs to be considered in interpretation. It is possible that if High

Figure 5.3. Rock art incorporated in a rock ring with ground stone in the foreground, High Basins, Nevada. Photograph by S. W. Pendegraft

Basins rock art predates subsequent domestic occupation, it may have attracted subsequent populations to make their campsites there. These subsequent groups may have incorporated High Basins rock art into their traditions in ways that left no archaeological trace, though closer attention to the art itself may reveal signs of retouching (see Woody 2000a, 2000b, for further details of this argument).

Temporal or spatial distanciation of rock art from domestic routines positions the art in the field of male ritual discourses. Overlooking the art's domestic context allows the possibility that the art negotiated its presence amid female *and* male routines to be ignored in favor of interpretations emphasizing male agency. As the archaeology of High Basins rock art makes clear, such a construction of the field of discourse in which rock art was embedded is unwarranted.

The presence of rock art centrally located in the daily domestic routines of both men and women poses a challenge to a shamanistic interpretation of High Basins rock art, at least as far as this approach is currently theorized in the Desert West (Whitley 1994c, 1998a). If male shamans were making rock art at remote vision-quest locales as a record of their trance experiences (as the shamanistic model theorizes), it is difficult to accommodate the abundant domestic archaeology within this perspective. As noted above, temporally distancing the rock art and settlement archaeology in the High Basins is problematic, and it seems more economical to devise interpretations that incorporate women as agents in the making and use of rock art than it is to explain away evidence of their presence. Exploring the possibility of women's rock art at least supplements previous research that has concentrated on rock art as a male cultural product (Cannon and Woody [chapter 4], this volume).

Locating Women and Men Through High Basins Archaeology

The routines of daily life are one of the contexts in which identities and social practices are constructed and negotiated (Giddens 1984). Because resource use and processing technology are directly embedded in daily routines, such routines are potentially ethnically specific (Schneider 1993:15). In Great Basin archaeology both have been used to identify different cultural groups (Aikens and Witherspoon 1986; Bettinger and Baumhoff 1982). Likewise, rock art is potentially a "sensitive indicator of group affiliation and group identity when it serves as a method for symbolizing group boundaries" (Garfinkel 1982:67). As Layton (2000b) demonstrates, this is particularly true of art embedded in totemic theories of being, which use animal imagery as signifiers of corporate and kinship relationships and concepts.

Exploring the kind of archaeology with which High Basins rock art is associated sheds light on the social and economic routines that surrounded its use. Evidence indicates that logistical use of the High Basins occurred in the last 3,500 years with more intensive logistical and seasonal occupations occurring in the 1,000 or so years (Delacorte 1997:i, 150–55; Rusco 1981:9–10).

While the sexual division of labor is but one form of social classification, it is one of the most general and widespread. Its study is viewed here as having continued relevance and importance to understanding prehistoric lifeways. Women tend to concentrate on activities closer to households, and on subsistence resources that are more reliable, especially during their childbearing years (Elston and Zeanah 2002; Jochim 1988). Therefore, I use the division of labor as a tool to extract clues to understanding the motives for activities that could have contributed to the making of High Basins rock art. Sexual division of labor does not necessarily imply status differences or mutually exclusive economic tasks (Kent 1998), because social and economic organization are flexible given certain environments, activities, or times of the year.

The occupational debris in the High Basins approximates Binford's seasonal field camps on the forager-collector continuum (Binford 1980). The setting of the High Basins yields two resources necessary for a predominantly female seasonal plant processing camp—plants themselves and an abundant tool stone source for grinding, either on bedrock milling slicks or on milling stones locally quarried from basalt. It should be remembered that although the processing of plant resources is likely to have been primarily a female task, the role of men in gathering plant resources has often been underestimated. Research from California regarding the Milling Stone Horizon has produced evidence that decenters hunting and emphasizes female *and* male labor in plant gathering (Fitzgerald and Jones 1999; Jones 1996). Hence, although I envisage the High Basins settlement archaeology as the product of a predominantly female seasonal task force, men would also have been present at times.

These seasonal camps would have been the locus of parenting, occasional hunting forays, plant processing, and cultural activities such as singing, dancing, myth telling, and rock art use. Ethnographically, some painted body designs in the western Great Basin were sex-specific for distinct activities (d'Azevedo 1986:482), while other designs were specific to the sex of a baby (Fowler and Liljeblad 1986:449), suggesting that art in general, and rock art more specifically, was interpreted in part according to the sex of the observer. Because the High Basins rock art is situated in the midst of daily and economic social routines, with a predominantly female audience, it may have been used to explore and negotiate themes relating to sexual identities and economic reproduction. Since rock art is permanent and has an audience in perpetuity, like other prominent land-scape monuments it can be reinterpreted and incorporated by succeeding cultural groups (Bradley 1993, 1997). Their readings of rock art may be suggested by understanding the activities that took place around it.

This chapter situates women and their labors in the archaeological record and decenters imagery as the only source of understanding rock art's cultural functions. Ethnography demonstrates that identifying the sexual division of labor from archaeology is problematic, and certainly one should be circumspect in making broad characterizations such as "only men make stone tools" or "only women do the cooking" (Jones 1996; McGuire and Hildebrandt 1994). Ethnography and archaeology demonstrate that hunting and gathering was the primary form of economic organization in the Great Basin, with a generally egalitarian social order. This form of socio-cultural organization does not suggest a priori assumptions of special-ized social positions and therefore gives no reason to exclude women or their household members as potential creators of rock art. The presence of women in association with High Basins rock art fits the data of settle-ment archaeology better than separating women from the rock art and assuming that this form of symbolic culture is more strongly associated with male activities and/or themes. Many extant hunter-gatherers have sexual divisions of labor that vary spatially and seasonally for exploitation of certain resources, and this was probably also the case in the Middle and Later Archaic in the High Basins, especially regarding the more logistically oriented seasonal field camps.

When rock art is privileged and other archaeology is ignored or dis-sociated from the art by means of temporal or spatial displacement, questions arise because of the disparities in the evidence. Such distancing or displacing is parallel to the process whereby women are displaced as authors or users of art. Current theories emphasize the role of male ritual specialists in using rock art to negotiate statuses within groups of males, yet the art is frequently located in the center of domestic activities, and in some cases placed directly in house rings. Did the women not see this art or were they merely passive witnesses to male appropriations and uses of it? Or are modern archaeologists adopting the customs of their Baruya brothers (of Papua New Guinea), who lived in denial of the fact of female rituals (Godelier 1986)? Without consideration of the evidence of milling equipment, the availability of plant resources, and the contemporaneity of residence and rock art in the High Basins, it would be too easy to deny female agency in the making and use of the art.

CHAPTER 6

A Regional Settlement System Approach to Petroglyphs

Application to the Owyhee Uplands, Southeastern Oregon

MYRTLE P. SHOCK

Archaeological interpretations of rock art imagery have tended to focus on methods of production and subjective readings of the art's apparent references and to neglect the role of rock art in the experience of daily life. I argue that interpretation can be enhanced by viewing rock art as an archaeological feature that occurs in conjunction with other material culture and by considering rock art's broader landscape context as part of the larger settlement system. An approach to rock art based upon a synthesis of landscape and settlement system archaeology can be used to gain an understanding of the activities and social practices associated with rock art production and use, even in the absence of "informed" sources of understanding (Bradley 1997:214, 2000:79). An examination of rock art's landscape context potentially makes archaeologically visible the routines of daily life wherein identities and a sense of place are constructed and exposes rock art's relationship to them. The focus of this chapter is petroglyph sites in the Owyhee uplands of southeastern Oregon (see figure 1.1), where rock art commonly co-occurs with other archaeological features. The activity of petroglyph production occurred at locations where plant procurement and hunting also took place, and rock art and other archaeological sites share a similar regional distribution pattern. Using the concept of place provides a path to interpret rock art's cultural context by linking the activities that co-occurred with rock art creation and the probable social context of site use. The residential context of petroglyphs from the Owyhee uplands indicates that if they were created during religious or ceremonial activities, these activities were not spatially removed from subsistence activities and residence, and instead were publicly visible social rituals occurring within residential locations.

HUNTER-GATHERER LANDSCAPES OF ROCK ART

Rock art, as observed by archaeologists, is a palimpsest of the creative actions of individuals over time. It obviously had the capacity to hold symbolic meaning for its creators. An understanding of its significance, however, is dependent upon intersubjectivity as described by Layton (2000a). For archaeologists this shared subjective interpretation related to the understanding of art is rarely accessible. Since an "archaeologist cannot interact with the artists to discover what are the appropriate choices to make in any situation all (s)he can do is plot the accumulated choices made by the artists over time. We can show that certain references are appropriate in certain contexts" (Layton 2000a:52).

The fact that there were appropriate social contexts for rock art, and perhaps specific subsites of rock art, suggests that archaeologists may be able to assess interpretations of rock art on the basis of where it occurred within society.

If it is not random, the distribution of figures in the landscape has an indexical quality, pointing to some significance in the site. The fact that rock art remains where it was made provides the archaeologist of rock art with potentially significant information about context. If rock art is transferred, over time, from open-air to cave sites; if a given motif occurs at all sites during one period, but later becomes site-specific, these changes in context may reasonably be inferred to refer to changes in cultural significance. (Layton 2000a:52)

Archaeologists have a tendency to focus on contextual changes as indicators of cultural change. However, change and continuity of design styles, as well as the contextual location of rock art, assist in the interpretation of societies. The theoretical jump from the creation of one image to the cultural role of rock art is made on the basis of patterning in the accumulated rock art created by many individuals and the realization that individuals within a society had the opportunity to experience the intersubjectivity that is unavailable to an archaeologist (Layton 2000a). Because of this, the chronological history of rock art styles should not be divorced from the study of rock art because any breaks in rock art production could result in a loss of understanding of a shared meaning in rock art and possibly result in changes to the context within which rock art was created (Bradley 1997). Additionally, I argue that rock art and its chronology should not be divorced from the rest of the archaeological record. The creation of rock art is linked spatially to subsistence, mobility, and residence activities. Correlations can be observed only when rock art is considered contextually within the broader patterns of settlement (see also Cannon and Ricks [chapter 8], Cannon and Woody [chapter 4], Pendegraft [chapter 5], this volume).

Taçon and Chippindale have argued that rock art can be studied in two principal ways, through informed methods or formal methods. Informed methods allow the insight from pictures to be "passed on directly or indirectly from those who made and used the rock-art—through ethnography, through ethnohistory, through the historical record, or through modern understanding known with good cause to perpetuate ancient knowledge" (Taçon and Chippindale 1998:6). While informed methods can provide direct insight into an interpretation and the social role played by rock art, the use of informed methods for understanding rock art creation is often limited because ethnographic or ethnohistoric records are lacking or incomplete. In formal methods "the information available is then restricted to that which is immanent in the images themselves, or which we can discern from their relation to each other and to the landscape, or by relation to whatever archaeological context is available. This includes inference by location in landscape" (Taçon and Chippindale 1998:7–8). Formal methods have a great appeal to archaeologists. A body of literature that presents formal methods for rock art interpretation is landscape archaeology.

While the perspectives and themes covered by landscape research are broad, the goal of the pursuit is to relate human interactions to the environment (Ashmore 2004). Landscape context is potentially an important source for understanding the meaning of a site (Bradley 2000; Tilley 1994). Places derive their meaning from memory, recurrently performed activities, and ritual (Ashmore 2004; Tuan 1977). The people who attach meaning to places are the ones who are utilizing these places. Therefore, it is likely that the activities associated with rock art production were not separated from the routines that took place nearby or in direct association (Quinlan and Woody 2001, 2003; see also Cannon and Ricks [chapter 8], Cannon and Woody [chapter 4], Pendegraft [chapter 5], this volume).

It is important to differentiate between a view of landscape that divides space into cities or towns and the view of landscape that a hunter-gatherer might have had. According to Ingold (1986), hunter-gatherer territories are often conceived of in terms of sites and paths. Mobile groups would, therefore, lay claim to resources and territory based on trails that people used and vistas across the landscape. Archaeological sites were places within a web of frequent movement where meaning was tied to the activities that were engaged in, as well as memories of previous times when the activities had occurred.

ROCK ART IN A REGIONAL SETTLEMENT SYSTEM

The connections that landscape archaeology forges between places people used and their conceptions of such places must be based on archaeological data. Regional settlement system analysis can deal with describing and explaining variability in the archaeological record; therefore, it is a good practical method upon which to build the data sets helpful in interpreting rock art contextually. A regional settlement system approach to rock art draws on concerns of both landscape archaeology and settlement patterns. This integration of perspectives is accomplished by considering rock art in three ways: as a feature class, as a site component, or as a regional location. Rock art is a feature left by past peoples. Considering rock art as a site feature allows for quantification and application of standard archaeological techniques for analysis. For those archaeologists who wish to interpret the "meaning" of rock art, however, recording and quantification seem inadequate, and instead only "informed methods" offer the information necessary to produce interpretive accounts (Lewis-Williams 1998). In practice, this approach has led to rock art imagery becoming the primary focus of interpretation, with site contexts (when considered) being used as a further aid to interpret the ostensible references of rock art's symbolism (Heizer and Baumhoff 1962). Such an approach needs to be supplemented with one that contextualizes rock art at a site level to determine the activities that co-occur with its production and use, and at a regional level the location of petroglyph sites must be related to their context within the settlement system (Bradley 2000:39). As rock art formed a portion of the landscape for prehistoric inhabitants, it would be misleading for interpretation not to consider its context of associated activities and physical landscape properties.

At a regional level, rock art sites can be considered to be one type of site among many. Combining knowledge about archaeological sites with rock art and those without it can provide a better understanding of the rock art itself, in part because such a typology prioritizes rock art over other site attributes. Rock art was not created in a void, separate from other cultural activities; the integration of rock art research into settlement pattern study allows for understanding rock art production as part of a prehistoric settlement system. The activity of making petroglyphs was related to other activities that had roles within a settlement system and influenced the inhabitants' conception of place. The locations where rock art occurs can be contrasted and compared to those in a region where it does not occur. At a site level, rock art production may be one activity at a multi-activity site or the only activity occurring at a site. The activities and physical landscape that occur in conjunction with rock art—which may be represented by lithic scatters, rock features, caves, and water sources— provide important clues for determining the context of rock art creation. The activities that consistently occur at a series of rock art sites provide a basis for placing rock art within the settlement system and understanding the activity of making rock art. This regional approach to sites with rock art can provide evidence for the interpretation of the rock art on both the regional level and the site scale, using only archaeological data; it does not require subjective interpretation of rock art images. This approach precludes neither comparison between rock art types and designs that occur at different sites or within distinct site areas nor subjective interpretation of rock art.

In order to contextualize rock art at a single site and to compare rock art sites with non–rock art sites, researchers must identify similar characteristics of each, perhaps including site size, artifact feature classes, amount or density of features, ecological zone, and distance to water. Such characteristics can provide the basis for regional comparisons of site density, site size, and associated features. The activities that occurred in association with the creation of rock art can provide a basis for understanding the social role of rock art and the audience that viewed the art. One goal of such inquiry is to determine whether rock art was created alongside residential activities, at locations of social aggregation, or at "special-purpose" sites used only for rock art. Presence or absence of co-occurring activities can provide a basis for testing interpretive hypotheses. By addressing which activities co-occurred with rock art production, a researcher can determine not only the context in which rock art occurs but also whether it appears consistently within a single social context or in multiple contexts.

An analysis of the ecological setting with respect to such features as the presence (or absence) of a perennial water source, edible flora, and fauna can provide information on associated activities, as well as seasonality of rock art production (see Cannon and Ricks [chapter 8], this volume). The specific aspects of ecological setting that are valuable and consistent over prehistoric time vary by region.

At individual sites, the issue of contemporaneous activities comes to the forefront. It is important to gauge whether the rock art and other material culture were created at the same time or if site usage shifted over time. Optimally this information could be obtained by relative dating in the archaeological record. In the absence of dating, however, the theory that places acquire meaning through the repeated activities that were performed there can provide another avenue to interpretation of rock art. Since we expect mobile foragers and hunters to have performed the same actions for the same purposes at a site over time, we may be willing to assume that the suite of activities that co-occurred with rock art creation did not vary substantially.

ARCHAEOLOGICAL CONTEXTS OF ROCK ART

The interpretations of rock art suggest specific social contexts for the activities that resulted in the creation of designs. Therefore it is possible to extrapolate expectations for the context of rock art from proposed interpretations. These expectations can include ideas about design content, associated site activities, and the placement of archaeological sites within a settlement system. The landscape context of rock art provides a guide to understanding its intended audience and thus the kinds of social concerns it addressed (Bradley 2000:69). For example, sites with domestic associations would seem to have very different kinds of audiences (or users) than those located in remote areas and not associated with other aspects of settlement archaeology (see also Quinlan and Woody 2003; Cannon and Ricks [chapter 8], Cannon and Woody [chapter 4], and Pendegraft [chapter 5], this volume).

Ingold's (1986) interpretation of territoriality for mobile groups requires some system of marking boundaries in the landscape, and rock art could be a method by which such communication could have been achieved. The essential feature of this type of rock art is that it served as a medium for people who visited places at different times to communicate with each other (Bradley 1997:7). This possible role of rock art can be investigated by an approach that considers both the context and the audience of rock art: "Provided it was a means of communication, the two should be connected systematically. We cannot claim to read those messages today but we can consider the contents of rock art as information of greater or lesser complexity. In the same way, we cannot specify the exact composition of the group to whom that information was addressed, but we can say something about the likely character by considering where those messages were located in the landscape" (Bradley 1997:9).

Another hypothesis is that some rock art sites are aggregation locations. Conkey (1980) envisioned rock art as occurring at sites of seasonal population aggregation. At these locations rock art would serve a social role in ritual activities, such as initiations and marriages, which took place when a larger population came together. The structure of aggregation includes duration of occupation, the area of occupation, the social contexts, such as ritual and subsistence, and the individuals involved (Conkey 1980:612). Archaeologically, aggregation sites could be identified by size, location in an area with many resources, or the many artifact feature types associated with a greater range of activities.

In contrast to sites of aggregation, "special-purpose" sites might be expected to be relatively small, situated away from the main areas of settlement (and therefore archaeologically recognizable by a location in areas with sparse archaeological sites), and possibly in an area with few resources. Shamanistic "special-purpose" sites have been described as physically isolated or relatively inaccessible (Quinlan and Woody 2001:215). Archaeologically, "special-purpose" sites could have a variety of characteristics; it would be expected, however, that their features would differ from those of residential sites. In the case of a shamanistic site, if its intended audience was restricted, the site might be remote, have a small spatial area, and be difficult to access because of its landscape context.

THE OWYHEE UPLANDS

The landscape approach outlined above provides an "informing context" to interpret and understand rock art data collected in 2000 and 2001 by the author in the Owyhee uplands, Oregon. The Owyhee uplands are a semiarid region of southeastern Oregon (see figure 1.1), which makes up approximately two-thirds of Malheur County, Oregon. The Bureau of Land Management (BLM) is the largest landholder in the county, managing 63 percent of the 6.35 million acres, and almost the entire Owyhee uplands. Twenty-five petroglyph sites were located using BLM cultural resource records and the accounts of local inhabitants.

Rock art from the Owyhee uplands was examined as part of a regional settlement system. Little is known about the origin of the rock art or the identity of the people who made it. Viewing rock art sites as components of the settlement system provided the data for exploring both the activity of making petroglyphs and possible interpretations.

The groups who resided in the Owyhee uplands ethnographically were Northern Paiute and Northern Shoshone (Stewart 1939). No ethnographic record exists for the creation of rock art by the Northern Paiute or Shoshone in neighboring areas (Steward 1941, 1943; Stewart 1941), though for a contrasting view see Whitley (1994a, 1994c, 1998c) and counterarguments by Hedges (2001) and Quinlan (2000a, 2000b, 2001). Prehistoric inhabitants were probably also mobile foragers and hunters. However, the time depth to which the ethnographic record can be projected is unknown because of the ongoing debate about when Numic languages spread within the Great Basin (Madsen and Rhode 1994; Miller 1986). Archaeologically, the Owyhee uplands have few excavated sites and have been surveyed only sporadically. While projectile point chronologies exist, no cultural chronology has been established (Shock 2002). In short, avenues for informed methods of approaching rock art are closed because of the sparse ethnographic and ethnohistoric information.

Ecological Characteristics

The Owyhee uplands are a semiarid desert. Defined by the drainage of the Owyhee River and its tributaries, the Owyhee uplands are ecologically similar to the northern Great Basin (Murphy and Murphy 1986:285). Since the semiarid landscape of plateaus and canyons experiences no substantial accumulation or loss of sediment except along the rivers (Shock 2002), almost every archaeological site is a surface site and could plausibly represent any period of time throughout the last 10,000 years, with no stratigraphy.

The semiarid nature of the Owyhee uplands means that there are very few sources of perennial water. Current rainfall averages 20.9 centimeters (8.2 inches) annually (Western Regional Climate Center 2005). The landscape is dissected by intermittent drainages that flow only following rainstorms or snowmelt. Primary sources of perennial water are springs and the major rivers. In sum, water availability is quite low because access to major rivers is constrained by cliffs. The courses of rivers and streams have not changed significantly during the Quaternary (Andrefsky and Presler 2000), and locations of springs and natural water holes have likely been consistent for a long period of time.

Vegetational distributions are shaped by the low quantities and infrequency of water availability. The primary plant community is basin sagebrush scrub and perennial bunchgrass (Smith et al. 1997). Other plant communities include playa vegetation, sagebrush on lava beds, and the high-elevation community, which features mountain big sagebrush scrub and both mahogany and juniper woodlands. Depending upon soil depth and elevation, different subspecies of sagebrush (*Artemisia tridentata, spp.*) flourish (Anderson, Borman, and Krueger 1998; Smith, Monson, and Anderson 1997). Paleobotanical research reflects an environment that has supported *Artemisia* steppe/desert scrub communities for the last 8,000 years (Smith, Monson, and Anderson 1997).

Throughout desert environments high spatial variability of plants occurs (Smith, Monson, and Anderson 1997). Edible species appear in patches where the moisture content or soil depth necessary for their growth is present. Vegetation can differ significantly between patches; those in proximity to one another may contain varying species composition. Despite the diversity of plants, edible plants are rare, for many edible plants depend on very specific local environmental conditions (Elias and Dykeman 1982). Camas (*Camassia quamash*) grows in wetlands but is known to exist in the Owyhee uplands only in patches along one drainage. Currant bushes (*Ribes aureum* and *Ribes cerium*), on the other hand, prefer moisture and very deep soils, which are found only at the base of rimrock. Other edible plants have their own environmental niches, but a common denominator is that wetter locations tend to support more varieties.

Another ecological attribute of the Owyhee uplands that may be relevant to the location of archaeological sites is the local winds. Winds that come up in the morning and evening across the plateau regions of the Owyhee uplands are controlled by topography and are driven by gravity and the heating and cooling associated with morning and evening, respectively (Christopherson 1997). In the evening, as layers of the surface cool, the cold surface air is denser and sinks, moving downslope across the mesa as a katabatic wind. The reverse happens in the morning, as the air at lower elevations warms and rises, pushing in the opposite direction across the mesa as an anabatic wind. The combination of high winds and cooking fires introduces the hazard of humans' accidentally starting brush fires.

The Owyhee uplands have none of the boundaries that are attached to stable patterns of settlements and fields. The region is unsuitable for agriculture, so even today the physical landscape is similar to what a mobile prehistoric inhabitant would have viewed.

Survey Methodology

It was difficult to find and select rock art sites to record in the approximately 4-million-acre Owyhee uplands. Before the author's research, the entire existing record of known rock art sites totaled fifteen locations. The author documented known locations of petroglyphs and found additional locations by using BLM notes that referred to "Indian drawings" and by following leads from accounts of local inhabitants. Personal communications with amateur archaeologists and river rafters led the author to believe that in addition to the twenty-five sites discussed herein, at least four undocumented rock art sites exist along the Owyhee River and its tributaries.

The author's survey of rock art sites recorded the location of each archaeological site with rock art, associated archaeological features, the ecological setting of the site, and specifics regarding the rock art (Shock 2002). A Global Positioning System (GPS) unit was used to record the location of each panel containing petroglyphs. The panels were measured and photographed, and the individual elements were described. As all sites had multiple boulders or rock faces with art, designs were recorded according to the rock face upon which they were located (2002). Rock art designs were described by style, size, line widths, orientation, and method of execution (for example, scratching or pecking). The author applied a consistent scheme of design quantification at all sites in order to avoid differences in counting.

Style has often been used as a method of categorizing rock art. Heizer and Baumhoff (1962) proposed a series of styles for Great Basin rock art linked to a chronology. While the validity of their chronology has been contested (Francis 2001), the styles themselves are a widely known method of identifying designs. The author used Heizer and Baumhoff's (1962) style names to describe Owyhee upland rock art without assuming that a chronology could be constructed on the basis of the styles. All rock art in the Owyhee uplands is in the form of petroglyphs.

In addition to the petroglyph sites that the author documented, a database of all known archaeological sites in the Owyhee uplands was compiled from state records in 2000. Data acquired during the field survey were used to contextualize rock art in the Owyhee uplands, while the database of all known archaeological sites was used as a basis for regional comparisons. Information for regional comparisons included site location and site density, vegetation complexes, and distance of archaeological sites to perennial sources of water.

PETROGLYPH SITES IN THE OWYHEE UPLANDS

Comparison at a regional level of the archaeological locations with petroglyphs and those without demonstrated that petroglyph sites occurred in similar locations to other archaeological sites (figure 6.1). Along the Owyhee River, where the concentration of petroglyph sites appears to be high, the concentration of all archaeological sites is similarly high. The perception of high site concentration is at least partially attributable to the more extensive surveying that has occurred along the Owyhee River corridor.

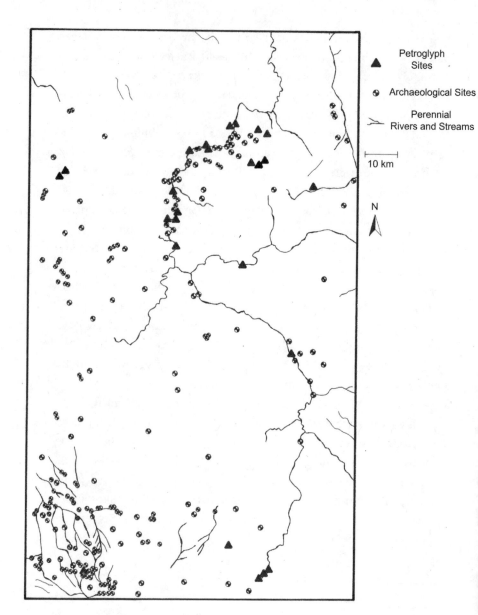

Figure 6.1. Relationship between rock art, other archaeological sites, and perennial water in the Owyhee uplands, Oregon. Drawing by M. Shock

An exception to petroglyph sites occurring in similar locations to other archaeological sites was observed in the Trout Creek Mountains (southwestern corner of the Owyhee uplands). This region has many archaeological sites but no known petroglyph sites. There are distinct differences in vegetation between the Trout Creek Mountains and other portions of the Owyhee uplands. The Trout Creek Mountains are in the mountain big sagebrush scrub, mahogany and juniper woodlands vegetation community, while the majority of the Owyhee uplands and all the petroglyph sites fall within the sagebrush and bunchgrass grasslands plant community.

All archaeological sites in the Owyhee uplands were examined to see if they were located within 1,500 meters of a perennial water source (see figure 6.1). Petroglyph sites were more frequently associated with perennial water than archaeological sites in general. Proximity to water is important in an arid region where it is a scarce resource. Eighty-four percent of petroglyph sites (21 of 25) in the author's survey were located within 1,500 meters of perennial water sources, as opposed to only 72 percent of all archaeological sites as compiled in the 2000 database (369 of 511). Activities associated with perennial water sources could have included fishing along rivers, hunting animals that came to water, or gathering plants that grow in wetlands.

In the Owyhee uplands, approaching rock art as part of the settlement system led to several observations. In terms of site size, 36 percent of petroglyph sites were larger than 2 hectares, whereas only 8 percent of reported non-petroglyph sites were larger than 2 hectares. Regional site distribution showed that petroglyph sites were found in locations similar to those where other archaeological sites were found, with the exception of the Trout Creek Mountains. On the basis of the current vegetation complex, petroglyph sites are located in only one vegetation community: sagebrush scrub and perennial bunchgrass grassland. Additionally, at the regional level petroglyph sites were found to occur more frequently within 1,500 meters of water than all archaeological sites did.

Owyhee Uplands Multipurpose Rock Art Sites

In general, Owyhee uplands archaeological sites have the chronological problems of being surface sites with no stratigraphic deposits and few datable artifacts (Shock 2002). Therefore, there is no evidence to suggest or refute particular activities' occurring within the same time frame.

TABLE 6.1 | Rock Art Sites and Associated Archaeology, Owyhee Uplands

CONTEXT	SITE NUMBER	ROCK ART VISIBLE FROM 100 METERS AWAY	PERENNIAL WATER SOURCE	ACCESS OF ANIMALS TO WATER	POTENTIAL FOR FISHING	GROUND STONE	LITHIC SCATTER	ROCK FEATURE	EDIBLE PLANTS	SHELTER FROM WIND	SHELTER FROM RAIN	DISTANCE TO WATER (METERS)	SITE AREA (HECTARES)
Water tub	35ML605											0	0.1
	35ML1054											0	0.1
	35ML688											0	0.2
Riverside	35ML105	+	+	+	+		+					15	0.25
	35ML130	+	+	+	+	+	+				+	10	0.5
	35ML144	+	+	+	+		+					15	0.04
	35ML153	+	+	+	+		+					0	0.1
	35ML156	+	+	+	+	+	+		+			15	8.1
	35ML168	+	+	+	+	+	+		+			25	5
	35ML197	+	+	+	+		+					20	0.01
	35ML164	+	+	+	+							10	0.1
	35ML196	+	+	+	+							10	0.01
	35ML692	+	+	+	+							100	0.4
Mesa top	35ML1057	+	+	+			+	+	+	+		5	0.05
	35ML1044	+	+	+			+	+	+	+		500	8
	35ML1045	+	+	+			+	+	+	+		0	9.4
	35ML1046	+	+	+			+	+	+	+		200	6.3
	35ML1050	+	+	+			+	+	+	+		25	25
	35ML1051	+	+	+			+	+	+	+	+	0	1.1
	35ML1052	+	+	+			+	+	+	+		400	14
	35ML842	+	+	+			+	+	+	+	+	50	5
	35ML850	+	+	+			+	+	+	+		800	10
	35ML1053	+	+	+			+	+	+	+	+	100	0.9
	35ML992	+	+	+						+		0	1.9
	35ML1049	+	+	+					+	+		800	0.05

(Shock 2002)

Since locations are ascribed meaning from the activities that occur at them (Moore 1986; Ricoeur 1981), however, the author examined activities at sites in the Owyhee uplands with the assumption that the activity of petroglyph making probably co-occurred with other activities. This is supported by the other archaeological features found at petroglyph sites in the Owyhee uplands: lithic scatters were found at 72 percent of the sites, rock features at 36 percent, ground stone at 12 percent, and rock shelters at 16 percent (table 6.1).

One site with rock art, 35ML1044, demonstrates how the archaeological and ecological setting can indicate the other activities that occurred at the location. This site is associated archaeologically with a lithic scatter of approximately 0.5 hectare and with rock walls (figure 6.2). In an ecological sense it is situated above a wetland and has a perennial water hole approximately 500 meters away. Edible vegetation on the hillside around the petroglyph faces and in the valley below includes Great Basin wild rye, currants, camas, biscuit-root, and wild onions. The location of petroglyphs on the rimrock at 35ML1044 coincides with where the rimrock provides a sheltered location from the wind; an unprotected fire would be subject to local winds.

The archaeological artifacts and ecological setting of 35ML1044 suggest that procurement of plant resources and hunting were activities that co-occurred with rock art production. The collection of plant resources is supported by the presence of otherwise scarce flora that are dependent upon wetlands or the deep soil that accumulates at the base of basalt rimrock. The author's personal observation determined that the wetland at 35ML1044 remains green after surrounding grassland and sagebrush steppe vegetation has died. This and a perennial water source would draw large game animals, specifically *Antilocapra americana* (pronghorn) in the middle to late summer when the semiarid landscape is parched (Shock 2002).

The artifactual remains and natural resources that co-occur with the petroglyphs at the site of 35ML1044 suggest that the location was used for hunting and the collection of plant resources in the context of temporary residential occupations. Water was available at a perennial water hole. The occurrence of petroglyphs on basalt rimrock, which also provided shade from the summer sun in the afternoon and shelter from the wind, puts

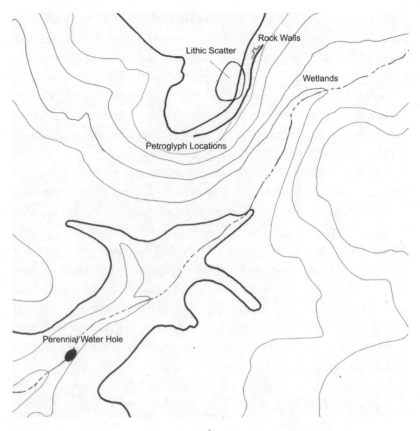

Figure 6.2. Landscape context of Site 35ML1044, Owyhee uplands, Oregon. Drawing by M. Shock

rock art firmly within the context of residential behaviors. The designs are in some cases visible from a distance of more than 100 meters and consequently were not hidden from segments of the social group that used the site.

With an understanding of the settlement system and the archaeological context of the petroglyphs at 35ML1044 it is possible to consider the fit of various interpretations. This site fits the expectations of neither an isolated "special-purpose" site (as would be associated with shamanic ritual) nor an aggregation location. While there are natural resources to support a population, they occur in the patch around the perennial water and in the deep soils below the basalt rimrock. It is therefore unlikely that a large population could have been supported for any extended period at

35ML1044, indicating that it could not have functioned as an aggregation locale. In moving to interpretations of boundary marking and hunting magic, the rock art at 35ML1044 does not differ in design content from other rock art within the Owyhee uplands; the majority of the images are abstract in nature (table 6.2). While 35ML1044 has fifty-five representational design elements (more than all other sites combined) these do not represent hunters and their game, such as might be expected of art functioning as hunting magic. The best interpretation of the activity of rock art creation at 35ML1044 is that which can be deduced from its context: rock art was created at a place where residential groups engaged in the procurement and processing of everyday resources, both plant and animal.

The Three Site Contexts

Within the Owyhee uplands, the activity of making rock art was not isolated from other activities carried out by native inhabitants. The fact that rock art production co-occurred with other archaeological features is a pattern seen throughout the Owyhee uplands. Rock art sites occur in three specific contexts within the settlement system (Shock 2002). The pattern of activities in which people were engaged at 35ML1044 typifies the mesa top context (figure 6.3). The other contexts in which petroglyphs occur have been labeled water tub and riverside (see table 6.1).

Water tub petroglyph sites have a few petroglyphs located on boulders around a natural water catchment. Of the three sites, only one is associated with another archaeological feature, a lithic scatter. Water tub features function as catchment basins for water after rainstorms or snowmelt. These sites, as locations in the landscape, are possible stopping spots in an otherwise barren and dry land. All of these sites are located between areas with access to water, either far from rivers or separated from them by cliffs.

Riverside petroglyph sites are located along the two major water sources, the Owyhee River and Jordan Creek. While these cut deep canyons with sheer cliffs, petroglyph sites are found where intermittent drainages create a more gradual slope and a broad terrace. Only a small percentage of the sites found along the Owyhee River and Jordan Creek have petroglyphs. These eleven riverside petroglyph sites are characterized by lithic scatters, some ground stone and rock shelters, and the potential for fishing. These

TABLE 6.2 | Types of Rock Art Styles Present at Owyhee Uplands Rock Art Sites

SITE NUMBER	ABSTRACT	REPRESENTATIONAL	PIT AND GROOVE	SCRATCHED	DOTS
35ML153	45		2		23
35ML605	18	2			
35ML688	173	8			41
35ML850	102			13	10
35ML1044	214	55		10	16
35ML1045	493	11		5	74
35ML1046	39	4			4
35ML1050	125		10		16
35ML1051	242	3		3	15
35ML1052	90				17
35ML1053	29	1			12
35ML1054	15	2			
35ML1057	15	4			3

(Shock 2002)

sites appear to be primarily residential, and they may have been aggregation sites, since the terraces could accommodate a large gathering and fish might have been an abundant resource at the time the sites were occupied.

The context of all mesa top petroglyph sites is very similar to the specifics of 35ML1044, which have been described above. The resources at these sites for a prehistoric population would be seasonally available edible plants and the animals that came to drink at perennial water sources (see table 6.1). These resources are typical of a seasonal residential camp. While mesa top petroglyph sites were found at locations that could be used for hunting, hunting magic is not a likely interpretation of the petroglyphs. The residential context of these petroglyph sites is a much more consistent theme and probably relates to the social role that the petroglyphs played.

The fact that petroglyphs occur in three different site contexts in the Owyhee uplands indicates that petroglyphs possibly played multiple social roles. Therefore, it is not possible to assign one global role to the art; rather, the specific contexts must be explored. The water tub petroglyph sites occur in a context where little can be said about associated activities except the availability of seasonal water. The other contexts in which Owyhee upland petroglyphs occur provide a greater wealth of information on the possible social role of rock art. The mesa top and riverside contexts are residential in nature but have different possible resources. If riverside sites were used for

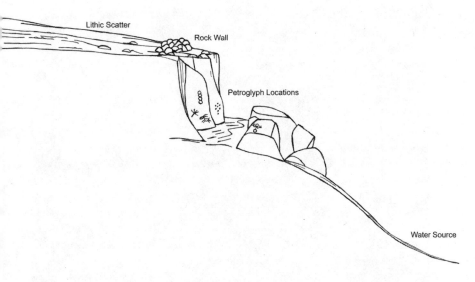

Lithic Scatter

Rock Wall

Petroglyph Locations

Water Source

Figure 6.3. Diagrammatic profile of an Owyhee uplands mesa top petroglyph site type. Drawing by M. Shock

fishing, it is possible that they could have supported an aggregated population. Additionally, riverside sites are on wide flood plains with space for a relatively large number of people simultaneously, whereas the mesa top sites possess no single resource that would draw people together. In both contexts rock art is highly visible and would be accessible to all members of society who frequented the resources. In terms of the possible role of rock art as boundary communication, petroglyph sites in the Owyhee uplands were positioned not to overlook the landscape or mark a trail, but rather at the actual location of productive resources. Petroglyph sites show use similar to that at other settlement and resource procurement locations.

Owyhee Uplands Petroglyph Design Categorization and Quantification

Petroglyphs in the Owyhee uplands were compared on the basis of site-by-site differences in the occurrence of different design types (see table 6.2). For Owyhee uplands petroglyphs, the different chronological periods that Heizer and Baumhoff (1962) designated for Great Basin rock art styles were not apparent. There were no regular instances of the superimposition or differing repatination that would have led the author to place these

Figure 6.4. Characteristic abstract
imagery in the Basin and Range
tradition, Owyhee uplands, Oregon.
Photograph by M. Shock

Figure 6.5. Anthropomorph,
Owyhee uplands, Oregon. Photograph by M. Shock

stylistic classifications into different chronological periods, even at petroglyph sites in the Owyhee uplands where abstract, representational, and scratched elements were all present.

In the Owyhee uplands, the majority of petroglyphs were created by pecking. Pecked petroglyphs take on a variety of forms (see table 6.2). The majority are composed of squiggly lines, meanders, or circular forms (figure 6.4). Another common design is dots. Representational petroglyphs account for less than 5 percent of the total designs (figure 6.5). The other method by which petroglyphs were created was scratching. Scratched designs tend to be composed of straight lines. Designs of many types are often found on a single basalt boulder. All of the known petroglyphs were made on basalt, so the designs are a light color against the dark basalt. In addition, petroglyph designs have varying degrees of patination, and single petroglyph designs are infrequently superimposed upon other designs.

Using data specific to rock art designs, one can take many avenues for formal methods of understanding rock art's role in social systems. One possibility is to calculate whether the rock faces on which the art was created were used equally, or if those at some sites were used more intensively. For each rock art site, the average number of designs found on each rock face was calculated (table 6.3). In the case of the Owyhee uplands, the number of designs per rock face varies considerably within single sites, but the differences in mean number of designs per rock face by site are not significant. Utilization of available rock canvas might vary considerably between rock art sites. This measure has intriguing possibilities if one site in a region was in some way "central" to rock art and had many more designs on the rock faces.

The Owyhee uplands lack the ethnographic record that would allow use of informed methods in interpreting petroglyphs. The formal methods based on landscape archaeology and settlement patterns have made it possible to propose ways of interpreting the rock art. The perspective that rock art is a constituent of archaeological sites rather than an entity unto itself is a viable formal method for analyzing rock art, especially when the way in which people formed connections to place is considered. Since rock art is the product of an activity engaged in by the prehistoric inhabitants of the Owyhee uplands, perceiving how its creation articulated with other

TABLE 6.3 | Designs Per Rock Face in Owyhee Uplands Rock Art Sites

SMITHSONIAN NUMBER	NUMBER OF FACES	NUMBER OF ELEMENTS	ELEMENTS PER FACE (1 STANDARD DEVIATION)
35ML153	33	107	7.0 ± 8.0
35MLL605	11	42	4.0 ± 1.8
35ML688	6	17	3.8 ± 4.1
35MLL850	7	22	6.0 ± 4.0
35ML1044	10	70	3.7 ± 3.1
35ML1045	5	20	3.5 ± 3.2
35ML1046	59	223	2.4 ± 2.0
35ML1050	21	125	3.0 ± 2.8
35ML1051	79	259	4.6 ± 6.1
35ML1052	163	584	3.2 ± 2.1
35ML1053	21	50	3.8 ± 2.3
35MLL1054	50	153	2.8 ± 2.1
35ML1057	57	263	3.1 ± 2.3

(Shock 2002)

activities allows for better understanding of the social contexts. As such, these formal methods can be both an alternative approach and a complementary approach to interpreting rock art from designs.

This chapter incorporates three levels of analysis to better understand the context of rock art in the Owyhee uplands: at the regional level site types and distribution can be examined; at the site level the activities occurring at a single site can be determined; and at the design level rock art is quantified and categorized as a feature. At the regional level the distribution of petroglyph sites was observed to be similar to the distribution of all archaeological sites, while more petroglyph sites were found to be close to sources of perennial water. This distribution of petroglyph sites indicated that the setting preferred for rock art was the same as that for residential camps. Examining petroglyphs as a component of the archaeological site provided evidence for activities that occurred in conjunction with the creation of petroglyphs. Petroglyphs were made at multipurpose sites, like 35ML1044. Sites of this type were probably places for hunting and collection of edible plants, as well as creating rock art. At the design level petroglyphs from throughout the Owyhee uplands were found to conform to basic principles of design, the majority being abstract in nature. Additionally, none of the locations were used more intensively than others in terms of designs made per panel of basalt.

The desert environment of the Owyhee uplands eliminates the reconstruction of temporal depth at most surface archaeological sites, but it also makes water and edible plants scarce resources. Therefore, the association of rock art with locations that have sparse resources and abundant artifacts indicates that these locations were likely used repeatedly for the resources, if nothing else. While we do not know exactly how the prehistoric inhabitants conceptualized these places, the rock art was integral to the sense of place and the construction of meanings of place.

Within the Owyhee uplands petroglyphs did not occur in a single context, but rather in three distinct contexts, termed mesa top, riverside, and water tub sites. The water tub sites probably served as stopping places in an otherwise dry landscape, suggested by the association of the locations that trap runoff. While these were not isolated locations, neither are water tubs at locations that would have been desirable for resource procurement. Riverside sites, in contrast, may have been associated with plentiful resources if riverine resources were exploited in conjunction with the creation of petroglyphs. Detailed analysis of these sites must await a better understanding of the riverine resources that were used (freshwater fish, anadromous fish, and mussels) and the specific riverine conditions used in their procurement. Of the interpretations proposed, it is possible that the creation of rock art at riverside sites occurred in the context of population aggregations. The mesa top sites were places where petroglyphs occurred within the social context of residential camps. These places have rich patches of edible plant resources and perennial water sources that would have drawn large game during the dry months. If ritual or religion were the driving force behind the creation of rock art, the context of these activities was alongside residence.

CHAPTER 7

The Study of a Rock Art Site in Southeastern Oregon

KEO BORESON

This study was made possible by the U.S. Bureau of Reclamation, Snake River Area Office, which contracted with Archaeological and Historical Services at Eastern Washington University to locate and document the rock art along a section of the Owyhee Reservoir in southeastern Oregon. About 160 acres were surveyed, 121 boulders with 137 panels of petroglyphs were documented, and an additional 115 rock art–bearing boulders were located. The 236 boulders with petroglyphs were designated as site 35ML1019 (Boreson 2002).

While the original intent of the work was to record the physical characteristics of the petroglyphs, the study also provided the opportunity to investigate the relationship between rock art and other prehistoric and protohistoric remains by identifying the spatial context of the rock art in the settled landscape and assessing the stylistic attributes of the petroglyphs. Luther Cressman alluded to the importance of this topic of research when he wrote: "Neither the presence of water nor the availability of food alone seems to account for the profusion [of designs] in the Owyhee Gorge.

To these factors must be added at least one more, safety from marauders. . . . Could the combination of these three factors—water, food, and safety—account for the marked development in this marginal area? Or was there some socio-psychological situation which was the real cause? This is a question which must go unanswered for the present and perhaps forever" (Cressman 1937:71).

THE PHYSICAL AND CULTURAL LANDSCAPE

The study area is a mostly north-facing landform with slopes that vary from nearly level to moderately steep. The present-day topography is the result of mass wasting of basalt rock from the south. Owyhee Reservoir forms the northern boundary of the surveyed area, and the original river channel is adjacent to some of the present-day shoreline. "Owyhee Reservoir is located in an area that is peripheral to both the Great Basin and Columbia Plateau geographic and cultural areas. Human occupation of this area began as much as 14,000 years before present (B.P.). . . . They practiced a mobile hunting and gathering lifestyle likely consistent with those practiced in the basin for many thousands of years. They occupied river valleys seasonally to harvest anadromous fish and plant foods. During other seasons, they foraged upland areas and streams" (U.S. Bureau of Reclamation 1994: 2–40, 2–42).

Steward (1938:figure 1) and Fowler and Liljeblad (1986:435) identify the occupants of the region as the Northern Paiute, although the Owyhee River drainage in eastern Oregon is near the linguistic boundary of the Northern Paiute and the Shoshone and was a zone of overlap used jointly by both groups (Fowler and Liljeblad 1986:435, 437, figure 1). People would gather seasonally at preferred camping places, and in most areas clusters of families would meet semiannually. At other times, individual households formed smaller camp clusters (Fowler and Liljeblad 1986:436).

During historic times the vicinity of the project became known as Watson, after a nearby post office established in 1898, which later moved 2.3 miles upriver. Watson Cemetery is also near the study area. Owyhee Dam was completed in 1932, and the reservoir inundated homes, fields, and petroglyphs along this stretch of the river. The last residents of Watson left the area in 1936, and at present recreation and livestock grazing are the main land-use activities.

In the early 1980s J. Malcolm Loring and Louise Loring (1983) recorded forty boulders with petroglyphs at this locale, of which twenty-two were documented during this project. A survey conducted by Archaeological and Historical Services in 1994–95 identified two petroglyph sites within the study area (Luttrell 2000), which subsequently provided data for part of Joe Randolph's master's thesis (Randolph 2001:iii, 101). Both of these sites were redocumented during this survey.

Several isolated finds were observed within the boundaries of site 35ML1019: nine flakes, six unifaces, a biface, a utilized chunk, a cairn, a talus pit, and two rock alignments. One rock alignment appears to be directly associated with rock art panel 88A, and the other might be related to rock art panel 47A, both part of the site. These artifacts and features are not indicative of the quantity and variety of items usually associated with habitation sites. The identified cultural remains do suggest that the study area was not used extensively except for creating petroglyphs, activities related to the rock art, and perhaps occasional hunting and gathering.

Although evidence for habitation was not found in the study area, at least five archaeological sites with artifacts suggesting temporary or long-term occupation are located between one and two miles from the project (Luttrell 2000). These are two rock shelters with low-density lithic and artifact scatters and, at a hot springs, a petroglyph site with high-density lithic and artifact scatters. The numbers and types of artifacts observed on the ground surface suggest that the latter represents a favored living area, although it is not known if the rock art and archaeological assemblages are contemporary.

METHODS

While fieldwork was in progress between April 28 and May 20, 2002, the crew experienced snow, rain, high winds, and temperatures ranging from freezing to the mid-nineties. During this time the reservoir level was dropping, and by the end of the fieldwork the original Owyhee River channel in this area was apparent (figure 7.1). Fieldwork was conducted by four archaeologists, who examined the surfaces of thousands of basalt boulders for petroglyphs (figure 7.2).

Large-scale aerial photographs were used to map the positions of the rock art–bearing boulders, and the locations were pinpointed with a

Global Positioning System (GPS) unit. The GPS data were downloaded to a portable computer every evening, and a generator was used to recharge the computer and GPS batteries. The data were later processed using Pathfinder Office 2.51, and corrected files were stored as ArcView Shapefiles for integration into GIS maps at the Bureau of Reclamation.

An IMACS Rock Art Attachment form was completed for each petroglyph panel. The petroglyphs were photographed with color slide and black-and-white print film and then traced onto four mil polyfilm. Black felt-tip pens were used to reproduce all of the peck marks, scratches, and abrasions made by humans. A few nondescript modified areas were treated as petroglyphs because of the context, such as when random-appearing peck marks were found near or on boulders with obvious designs. Natural impacts, such as cracked, exfoliated, and lichen-covered areas, were traced with red felt-tip pans. Subsequently, in the office, the tracings were reduced, scanned, and made report-ready. The fifteen largest tracings were photographed with a Nikon Coolpix 995 digital still camera, and the digital files were processed in Adobe Photoshop 6.0 before they were printed.

PHYSICAL ATTRIBUTES

Sixty-seven percent of the 137 panels are on south- or southwest-facing rock surfaces. No petroglyphs were observed on the north and northeast sides, where lichen growth is most abundant. No modification of prehistoric petroglyphs was observed, although there are three possible replicas of authentic designs. Patination was observed on 26 percent of the petroglyph panels. The most common natural impact, other than wind and rain, is caused by lichen growth, followed by spalling, bird perches, vegetation, and mineral deposits. Eight percent of the panels are affected by cultural impacts, including a boulder that is seasonally inundated and added names, initials, and letters.

Ninety-two percent of the panels have between one and ten figures, and 8 percent have between eleven and fifty petroglyphs. Superimposed forms appear on 7 percent of the panels; most common is stipple over solid pecking. The superimposed designs that could be identified are dots over dots, a horizontal wavy line over dots, a curvilinear design over a curvilinear design, and two historic additions. Natural features

Figure 7.1. View of a portion of the study area showing Owyhee River channel, looking west, May 15, 2002. Photograph by K. Boreson

that appear to be incorporated in the design are present on 19 percent of the panels, primarily involving forms on, parallel to, or over edges and cracks.

Stipple pecking was used on 48 percent of the panels, followed by stipple and solid pecking on 30 percent and solid pecking on 3 percent. Abraded and scratched designs, and combinations of these with stipple pecking, appear on 19 percent of the panels. The quantity, small diameters, proximity, and placement of some peck marks suggest that some petroglyphs were made with precision and specialized tools. Peck marks in pairs appear on 23 percent of the panels. Some of the paired peck marks have one mark that is relatively wide and deep adjacent to a mark that is smaller and shallower, suggesting that a relatively forceful tap was followed with a lighter, rebound tap. Peck marks with diameters of less than 1.0 mm were found on 9 percent of the panels, indicating that the punch had a very small bit. Strategically placed and separated peck marks were used on 20 percent of the panels, most commonly in linear and curvilinear designs.

Figure 7.2. View of slope in study area with Boulders 23–32, looking north-northeast. Photograph by K. Boreson

STYLISTIC ATTRIBUTES

The documented petroglyphs were grouped into seven categories, with eighteen stylistic elements. Of the 137 panels, 72 percent have designs that are in only one stylistic category and 28 percent have forms that fit more than one category. The petroglyphs with circular elements are most abundant, followed by rectilinear, curvilinear, and representational elements, respectively. Panels with multiple curvilinear and rectilinear forms and motifs, historic figures, and random peck marks are the least represented (table 7.1).

Circles are the most common stylistic element. This is followed by parallel lines, straight lines, intersected circles, curvilinear lines, curvilinear forms, historical figures, zoomorphs, anthropomorphs, connected circles, shield figures, curvilinear and rectilinear forms, multiple curvilinear and rectilinear motifs, dots, random peck marks, parallel arcs, spokes, and meandering lines. About half of the circles, straight lines, and parallel lines and all but one of the curvilinear forms are not directly

CATEGORY	PERCENTAGE (NUMBER)	STYLISTIC ELEMENT	PERCENTAGE (NUMBER)
Circular	32 (66)	circle	13 (27)
		intersected circle	9 (19)
		connected circle	5 (10)
		dots	3 (6)
		spokes	2 (4)
		parallel line	10 (21)
Rectilinear	19 (40)	straight line	9 (19)
Curvilinear	18 (38)	curvilinear line	8 (16)
		curvilinear form	7 (14)
		parallel arcs	2 (5)
		meandering line	1 (3)
Representational	14 (31)	zoomorph	5 (11)
		anthropomorph	5 (11)
		shield figure	4 (9)
Curvilinear and rectilinear	8 (17)	curvilinear and rectilinear forms	4 (9)
		multiple curvilinear and rectilinear motifs	4 (8)
Historical	6 (13)	historic figure	6 (13)
Random	3 (6)	random peck marks	3 (6)

(Boreson 2002)

associated with other petroglyphs. These are simple forms, particularly the circles and straight lines, which frequently are the only petroglyph on the boulder.

Circular Elements (N = 66)

Circles are present in twenty-seven panels. These take the shape of empty rings, a filled ring, incomplete rings, rayed circles, double circles, a triple circle, and a dot in the center of a ring. Circles in nineteen panels are intersected by a vertical line, a horizontal line, or crossed lines. Ten panels have connected circles that are clustered, chained, connected by a line, stacked, or attached to a central point. The four panels with spokes have lines radiating out from a hub. The dots in six panels have small circular areas of solid pecking that form lines, a square, a circle, and an arc.

An interesting comparison of intersected forms can be seen in figure 7.3, in which details from panel 36A and all of panel 119B are depicted (note that the detail from panel 36A is rotated 180 degrees to facilitate compari-

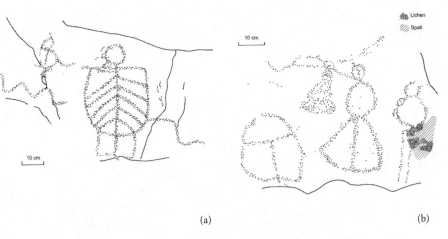

Figure 7.3. Comparison of intersected elements at Site 35ML1019, southeastern Oregon: (a) Panel 36A (detail—shown rotated 180 degrees); (b) Panel 119B. Drawing by K. Boreson

son). Each of these panels has an intersected form in the lower part of the central figure, and each is attached to a smaller object to the left of the head, one with an intersected circle and one that is triangular. Both panels also have an undulating line connected to the forms.

Rectilinear Elements (N = 40)

Nineteen panels have lines that are straight, crossed, or joined. Twenty-one panels have three or four parallel lines that intersect a U or V, an oval, or a square. Others have short lines that extend out from or intersect a vertical line, a horizontal line, a half circle, or an oval.

Curvilinear Elements (N = 38)

Curvilinear lines were identified in sixteen panels. These are simple undulating lines or curved lines that sometimes enclose an ovoid area or terminate at a circle or oval. Six panels are fairly distinctive in that they have an oxbow and a circle or oval at one or both ends (figures 7.4a–f). Fourteen panels have curvilinear forms that are curved, hook-shaped, or undulating. Five panels have parallel arcs with two or three curved lines. Three panels have a meandering line that is longer and straighter than the curvilinear lines.

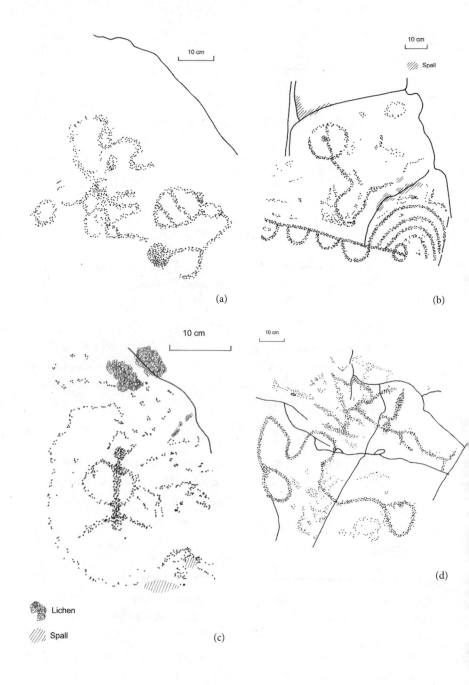

10 cm

(a)

10 cm

Spall

(b)

10 cm

10 cm

(d)

Lichen

Spall

(c)

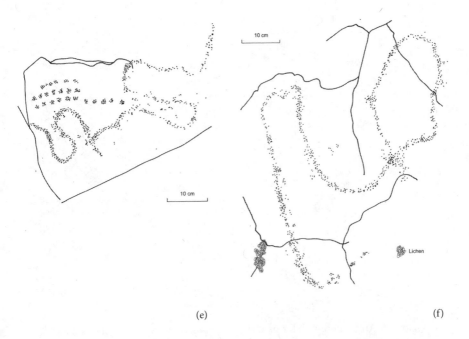

10 cm

10 cm

Lichen

(e)   (f)

Figure 7.4. Use of curvilinear elements in rock art panel compositions at site 35ML1019, southeastern Oregon: (a) Panel 47A (detail); (b) Panel 70A (detail); (c) Panel 74A; (d) Panel 100A; (e) Panel 110A (detail); (f) Panel 121A. Drawing by K. Boreson.

Representational Elements (N = 31)

There are eleven panels with zoomorphs depicting possible lizards, bighorn sheep, and deer or horses, eleven panels with anthropomorphs, and nine panels with shield figures. The most elaborate shield figure, in panel 120A, has a rayed head and is holding what appears to be a spear with a lanceolate point at the upper right and lines at the lower left. This form closely resembles a description of shield figures from the Montana High Plains:

> The more prominent elements . . . seem to be a circular design presumed to be a shield above which a person's head, and sometimes neck, appear. Legs and feet are shown except in rare instances. One of the more distinctive design elements is the lanceolate object resembling a coup stick that nearly always protrudes outward diagonally from the shield at ten o'clock or two o'clock. There are often feather-like objects which hang from the end of the lanceolate design. In a small minority

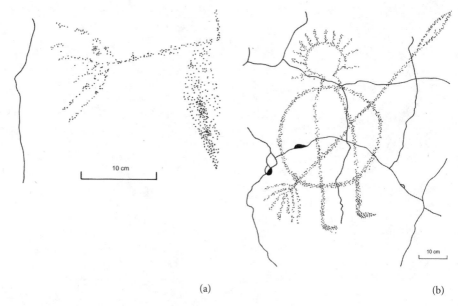

(a)   (b)

Figure 7.5. Anthropomorph forms at site 35ML1019, southeastern Oregon: (a) Panel
119A; (b) Panel 120A. Drawing by K. Boreson

of cases vertical lines seem to be intended to show the body of the warrior through the shield. (Conner and Conner 1971:14)

The shield figure in panel 120A is particularly interesting because a
petroglyph in panel 119A, about two meters upslope, appears to depict the
same spear with nearly identical lines on the left and a hanging lanceolate
point on the right (figures 7.5a–b).

Curvilinear and Rectilinear Elements (N = 17)

The nine panels with curvilinear and rectilinear forms are generally
vague and indistinct. The eight panels with multiple curvilinear and rectilinear motifs differ from those with curvilinear and rectilinear forms in
that the designs are more distinct, more abundant, and, in most cases, have
a greater variety of attributes.

Historical Elements (N = 13)

A few historical petroglyphs—including dates from the 1930s and a stipple
pecked house—appear to be related to activities in the study area of local interest.

In the area of located (but not documented) petroglyphs are additional words and names on boulders, including some that might be Spanish or Basque.

Random Elements (N = 6)

The six panels with random peck marks do not have recognizable designs.

COMPARISONS WITH REGIONAL ROCK ART STYLES

The stylistic elements of the petroglyphs in the surveyed area of documented petroglyphs strongly suggest ties with Great Basin Abstract Rock Art. This tradition "dominates and characterizes the Great Basin from the Sierra Nevada on the west to the Wasatch Range in central Utah on the east. It also occurs sporadically in adjacent areas including the Southwest and the Plateau culture areas" (Schaafsma 1986:215). The preponderance of circular elements in the project area, followed by rectilinear, curvilinear, and representational forms, fits with the characteristic types of Great Basin rock art described by Klaus Wellmann (1979):

> The circle and its elaborations constitute the largest class of all curvilinear abstract elements. Simple, bisected, sectioned, concentric, spoked, horned and tailed circles all occur with greater or lesser frequency, as do connected circles (including dumbbell shapes), circle chains, circle clusters, and circles with radiating lines ("sun disks") or with dots, bars, or other interior patterns. Also frequently encountered are ovals with parallel interior lines (oval grids), spirals, curvilinear meanders, and wavy or curved lines. More rarely seen are convoluted rakes, conjoined arcs, amoeboid forms, blocked ovals, and peltlike elements.
>
> ... Of the rectilinear forms, most often seen are rectangular grids, generally even-armed crosses, rakes, oblique cross-hatching (the hatched area may be enclosed), parallel straight lines, zigzag lines, and dots (single dots, groups and rows of dots, linked dots).
>
> The most commonly encountered representational motif in Great Basin rock drawings is the bighorn sheep (*Ovis canadensis*). (Wellmann 1979:56)

Although a few of Wellmann's diagnostic elements were not found in the study area, the overall assemblage is similar. One notable difference is the relatively few (two or three) petroglyphs portraying bighorn sheep, an observation that will more than likely be changed if casual identifications of quadrupeds in the area of located petroglyphs are verified.

An informal overview of illustrations of rock art from other sites in southeastern Oregon (Cressman 1937:36–39; Loring and Loring 1983:279–325) and southwestern Idaho (Erwin 1930:99, 101–10; Tobias 1981:17–46; Tuohy 1963:111–15) suggests that some, but not all, of the petroglyphs in the study area resemble the rock art in the greater region. There are also similarities to petroglyphs on the Snake River in Hells Canyon, where Leen reports five or six sites with pecked designs that contain "obvious similarities with numerous sites located in southern Idaho and throughout the Great Basin, and [which] can be classified as Great Basin Curvilinear Abstract" (Leen 1988:108–13, 188).

"Tentative and uncertain dates" suggested by Heizer and Baumhoff (1962) for the Great Basin Curvilinear Style are, roughly, 1000 B.C. to A.D. 1500. Superimposition of rectilinear elements over curvilinear elements indicates that, at least at one site, the rectilinear designs are not as old (Heizer and Baumhoff 1962:233, 311). More recent work using cation-ratio dating of patina from Coso Range petroglyphs "has yielded absolute dates that revise the earlier chronologies and suggests that petroglyphs in the Great Basin are almost twice as old as previously supposed" (Schaafsma 1986:220; see also Ritter, Woody, and Watchman [chapter 9], this volume).

Shield Figures

At least twenty-two shield figures were recorded in nine panels in the surveyed area. This stylistic element is widely distributed throughout the West. The motif is frequently a pictograph and there are many variations in the designs. Conner and Conner hypothesize that the motif is autobiographical, "that each was drawn by a warrior and shows him and his medicine shield" (1971:17). Shield figures are sometimes associated with depictions of horses, indicating that this form was used into the historic period. That this motif has survived for several centuries is supported by a radiocarbon date of A.D. 1104 associated with a rock art panel of shield-bearing warriors in south central Montana (Loendorf 1990:45).

This curious motif is identified with the Rocky Mountain region of the Southwest and Northern Great Plains regions. The northernmost record is from southeastern Alberta, south of Calgary. The major concentrations of the so-called classic shield figure are in Montana, northern Wyoming, and eastern Utah, though it occurs occasionally in southern Idaho, South Dakota, northeastern and central New Mexico, Arizona, northern Texas, and southern Nevada. (Grant 1967:61)

Shield figures are also found in Hells Canyon on the Snake River in west central Idaho (Leen 1988:94, 172), the Middle Fork of the Salmon River and the main Salmon River in east central Idaho (Boreson 1998:615), and the Camas Creek drainage in southwestern Idaho (Plew 1976:112).

The importance of this motif is, in part, linked to its widespread distribution, and considerable effort has been focused on explaining this through migration of or contact among prehistoric people.

The origins and pathways of diffusion of the shield motif are still very much a matter of controversy. Gebhard (1966) believes that it originated in central Mexico from where it was carried to the lower Pecos River region of Texas between A.D. 1 and 1000. It appeared next in the Fremont area of Utah (before A.D. 1150) from where it spread to the Great Plains (see also Keyser 1975). According to Gebhard (1966), further diffusion then took place into the Pueblo region of Arizona and New Mexico as well as to the cultures in the far west and in the eastern half of the United States. (Wellmann 1979:98)

Some provocative ideas emerged from assessing the physical data generated by this study. A wealth of information remains to be retrieved from site 35ML1019 and nearby areas, and recommendations regarding additional study are presented in the project report (Boreson 2002). The limited numbers and kinds of isolated finds observed within the boundaries of site 35ML1019 suggest that there was minimal prehistoric activity in the study area other than that related to the rock art. The association of one and possibly two rock alignments with panels of petroglyphs adds another dimension to future investigations here. The association of petroglyphs with abundant occupation debris at a hot springs less than two miles away provides an interesting contrast with site 35ML1019. Documenting the rock art at the hot springs site and comparing the physical and stylistic attributes with the petroglyphs at 35ML1019 might yield relevant information regarding the dynamics between areas used for habitation and rock art, particularly if the sites are shown to be contemporary.

The stylistic attributes of most of the petroglyphs documented at site 35ML1019 are solidly within the Great Basin tradition of rock art described by Wellmann (1979). The exception is the shield figure motif, which is found in many areas of the western United States. The shield figure in panel 120A, which bears such a strong resemblance to the motif in Montana described by Conner and Conner (1971), suggests influences from outside the Great Basin.

As Luther Cressman stated in the 1930s, the rock art in this region is a "magnificent elaboration of the Basin type" (1937:71). His observations and questions, cited at the beginning of this chapter, are as relevant today as they were almost seventy years ago. This is a unique and dramatic area for study, and with the right questions posed, perhaps answers will emerge.

CHAPTER 8

Contexts in the Analysis of Rock Art

Settlement and Rock Art in the Warner Valley Area, Oregon

WILLIAM J. CANNON AND MARY F. RICKS

Much has been made in recent years of the importance of ethnographic information in the study of rock art. Using ethnographic data collected from California and the Great Basin from the 1900s onward (Driver 1937; Steward 1938, 1941; Stewart 1941), Whitley has built complex interpretations of the art, including the reasons rock art was made, the ceremonies that accompanied the production of the art, and the use of the art in magico-religious ceremonies (Whitley 1992, 1994b, 2000a). He has argued that rock art was produced primarily by male shamans, often working in secret. Undeniably, ethnographic information can be useful if the native peoples who are consulted have taken part in the production of the rock art, or in rituals that involve the rock art. Ethnographic evidence is less compelling, however, in addressing rock art's original cultural contexts if the rock art is of great age or if there is no clear cultural connection between the producers of the rock art and those who are being consulted about its meaning.

Other researchers have suggested that Great Basin rock art was related to hunting, used as a magical aid to secure success in the hunt or to increase the number of game animals (Heizer and Baumhoff 1959, 1962; Nissen 1982, 1995). Others (Connick and Connick 1995) have proposed that some rock art was used to mark solar events, or as calendars. Schaafsma (1986:221) accepts the hunting magic association as a likely explanation for some Great Basin rock art, but notes that other rock art does not appear to fit with this interpretation. She concludes: "Both locational and graphic evidence exists to indicate that the rock art styles in the Great Basin culture area functioned in some capacity in connection with hunting ritual and in other shamanic contexts" (Schaafsma 1986:226).

Luther Cressman, of the University of Oregon, undertook a comprehensive study of rock art in Oregon in the 1930s. He found sixty rock art sites throughout the state, of which fifteen were in Lake County, and ten were in Warner Valley. He was convinced that "probably 90 per cent or more of the 'rock writings' in Oregon have been studied" (Cressman 1937:5). He noted: "With few exceptions living Indians deny knowledge of their meaning" (1937:4) and stated further: "Before there can be any hope of interpretation of the petroglyphs in a general sense as a phase of culture or for particular meaning, we must face the task of establishing an accurate record of their distribution both in extent and by types" (1937:8). Cressman urged the study of rock art as a part of culture and not as a thing unto itself: "To understand it, we must apply to it the scientific canons and methods of the ethnological study of the art of an era. . . . The difficulty in applying these methods is that we are often unable to find a temporal correlation of the petroglyphs with the other cultural products of the area" (1937:11).

Our work in a limited geographic area of the northern Great Basin has led us to believe that these theories, either singly or together, are insufficient to explain the corpus of rock art in our study region. We believe that the rock art of this area was created in public and was a part of daily life for sizable groups of people. We have undertaken analysis of the rock art within the context of the archaeological sites in which it is found. Further, we have considered the sites in terms of the valley ecosystem and the resources it offers to native people.

For nearly thirty years we have engaged in the recording and analysis of more than 250 rock art sites on Bureau of Land Management (BLM) lands in south central Oregon. The focus of this essay is a complex of 117 sites in Warner Valley and its surrounding uplands. More than two-thirds of these sites are concentrated in the south end of the valley, in an area of approximately 175 square kilometers.

Warner Valley lies in Lake County, in south central Oregon, just north of the point where the borders of Oregon, Nevada, and California meet (see figure 1.1). Several large lakes in the valley floor are remnants of Pleistocene Lake Warner. On the east side of the valley is the sharp rim of Poker Jim Ridge and Hart Mountain and their uplands, and the west side of the valley slopes gently upward to form the back slope of Abert Rim.

Lake County contains some of the oldest archaeological sites in the western United States. It has been inhabited, despite climatic fluctuations, since at least 10,000 B.P. (Bedwell 1970; Fagan 1974).

ETHNOGRAPHIC EVIDENCE FOR ROCK ART IN WARNER VALLEY

The people who inhabited Warner Valley at the time of Euro-American contact were Northern Paiute, whose language belongs to the Numic language family. The population in the Warner Valley area at the time of Euro-American contact, and the Native People with whom ethnographers consulted a century or more after contact, may not be related to those who inhabited the area long ago. It is likely that about 1,500 years ago these Northern Paiute, as part of the broader Numic dispersal (Lamb 1958; Madsen and Rhode 1994), replaced an earlier Desert Archaic population about which we know very little other than about their production of lithic artifacts. Ethnographic information dealing directly with the Warner Valley area and its occupants is limited and contains few references to rock art and its use or creation, a pattern repeated elsewhere in the Great Basin (Steward 1929:221–24).

Isabel Kelly worked with the Surprise Valley Paiute at Fort Bidwell, south of Warner Valley, in the summer of 1930. She also spent five days at the Klamath reservation, gathering what she called "scanty material" (Kelly 1932:67) from members of a band of Yahuskin Paiute from the area of Silver Lake and Summer Lake in northern Lake County. She describes a seasonal pattern in which hunting occurred year-round, while roots, fruits, berries, and seeds were gathered as they became available. She discusses the Paiute calendar and notes that "the calendar was definitely not regulated by or brought into accord with solar phenomena" (1932:153).

Kelly's description of Surprise Valley Paiute puberty rites mentions that the young men remained at home but were required to run each day for five days, during which time they abstained from eating game. Girls' puberty rites included a retreat to a menstrual hut during their first menses, where they stayed for a month. They also abstained from eating game. Women continued to retreat to the menstrual hut, where they remained for the duration of the menstrual period. Several women might occupy a hut, but men never approached them (1932:162–63). No mention was made of rock art in connection with puberty rites. Kelly notes: "Archaeological remains are fairly plentiful, although not spectacular, and are ascribed to mythical pre-Paviotso inhabitants. . . . Nümüna (people's father) is held responsible for petroglyphs" (1932:137).

Kelly's Paiute consultants told her that there were shamans among their people who cured illnesses and occasionally controlled weather. An antelope shaman officiated at ceremonial hunts. A few shamans were known by the consultants to prophesy (1932:189–90). Shamanic power was received through dreams, and usually came unsought, though it could be acquired by spending the night at one of several spots that were used for that purpose (Knack and Stewart 1984:27; Park 1938:110; Whiting 1950:29–32). There is no mention of the use of hallucinogens, but the dream-seeker fasted overnight. Both men and women could be shamans (Park 1938; Whiting 1950), and shamans had "limited situation-specific authority" (Knack and Stewart 1984:27).

Omer Stewart's (1941) description of Paiute culture included information from bands in the area of Burns (north and east of Warner Valley) and in the Fort Bidwell area. His consultants in these two bands knew that petroglyphs existed but had only heard about them and were not familiar with them from firsthand experience. The Fort Bidwell consultants told Stewart that Coyote made the petroglyphs, while those in the Burns area believed them to have been made by "Old-time" (non-Paiute) Indians (Stewart 1941:418). Some have interpreted this attribution of rock art production to Coyote as perhaps a metaphor of its perceived antiquity, particularly as Coyote was not a shamanic spirit helper among the Northern Paiute (Quinlan 2000b:99).

Couture discusses large upland gatherings of the Harney Valley Paiute in spring and summer, and notes that "other people . . . would join them from far away including Warm Springs Indians, Bannocks, Shoshone, 'Columbia River Indians,' Umatilla and Surprise Valley Paiutes. . . . During this time they re-established relationships, engaged in root digging, and trading" (1978:29). Couture, Ricks, and Housley (1986:158) suggest that "at predictable times of the year, plant gathering was a primary focus of activities, and that an examination of alternative adaptive strategies for exploitation of the environment may provide clues to the utilization of sites."

Some present-day Paiute with whom we have consulted talked of large gatherings in the uplands in spring and summer to procure and process roots, berries, and fruit. People from far away would join these gatherings, where in addition to preparation of food for winter storage, social activities took place, marriages were made, gambling was done, and races were held.

The rather limited ethnographic studies of Warner Valley inhabitants and their close neighbors provide no indications that these people made rock art, or that they were well informed about its manufacture or its uses.

ARCHAEOLOGICAL RESEARCH IN THE WARNER VALLEY REGION

Margaret Weide (1968) undertook a broad-based study of archaeological sites in the Warner Valley Basin for her doctoral dissertation. Using ethnographic data, she inferred that people gathered in winter at lowland lakeside sites and spent the spring, summer, and fall moving from place to place, exploiting resources as they became available. She states: "Camps in the uplands were used by small groups of people, and perhaps more usually by men than by whole family groups, suggested by the absence of grinding tools from many of the sites" (Weide 1968:245).

John Fagan (1974) conducted test excavations at several upland sites to test Stephen Bedwell's (1970:217) hypothesis that sites located at upland springs had been occupied during the posited Altithermal drought in the Great Basin (Antevs 1948:168–91). Fagan found that upland spring sites in Lake County, as well as those he tested in Harney and Malheur counties to the east of Warner Valley, showed evidence of occupation throughout the last 11,000 years. He stated that upland sites were hunting camps throughout this time period, basing this on the lack of milling stones observed at the sites.

More recent archaeological investigations in the Warner Valley conducted by the University of Nevada, Reno (Cannon et al. 1990) expand Weide's model to include settlement in the uplands as well as the lowlands. Lowland settlements were probably occupied by a substantial number of people in the winter months, and groups (including men, women, and children) traveled to the uplands in the spring to search for plants to eat fresh or to dry for the winter, as well as game animals.

Contrary to what was suggested by Weide (1968) and Fagan (1974), we have found a large number of grinding stones at upland sites, of varied ages, as indicated by degree of their repatination, which indicates to us that plant resources have drawn people to the uplands for thousands of years. Projectile points found at these sites show that the sites were occupied throughout the full span of occupation in the northern Great Basin.

Jenkins (2003) has compiled more than one hundred radiocarbon (^{14}C) dates from archaeological sites in the Fort Rock Basin in northern Lake County. These dates range from approximately 2800 B.P. to 13200 B.P., showing no breaks that might indicate human abandonment of the basin during the last 10,000 years.

THE WARNER VALLEY ROCK ART PROJECT

Before the formal archaeological programs on BLM lands (most of which were begun in the mid-1970s as a response to the National Environmental Policy Act of 1969 and the National Historic Preservation Act of 1966), a rather limited effort had been made to develop a list of archaeological sites within the boundaries of the Lakeview BLM District. These efforts were largely intended to record lithic scatters and occupation sites that contained projectile points; little attention was paid to ground stone artifacts at sites. Since projectile points were, and still are, a primary method of dating sites in the region, it is not surprising that the emphasis was on finding and recording points. Neither ground stone nor rock art is easily datable (see Ritter, Woody, and Watchman [chapter 9], this volume); thus each has often been ignored. We have revisited many of these sites, originally recorded by professional archaeologists. Their site reports have no mention of ground stone or rock art, but it was clearly present. In general, rock art was considered separately from other archaeological materials, if it was considered at all (see also Cannon and Woody [chapter 4], this volume). In a number of cases, rock art within archaeological sites was given a trinomial site number different from that of lithic materials at the same location, illustrating that the perceived separation between rock art and daily routines (Whitley 1998a:22) is in some cases the product of archaeologists, rather than an actual archaeological pattern, a theme also discussed by Pendegraft (chapter 5, this volume) and Quinlan and Woody (2003:374–75), and one that we have raised before (Cannon and Ricks 1986; Ricks and Cannon 1993).

In the late 1970s we began the process of recording rock art sites within the Lakeview BLM District. One of our concerns was to record data about the rock art in such a way that they might lend themselves to statistical analyses. We recorded more than one hundred variables for each site, including styles of art present, number and types of design elements, animal and plant communities at the sites, and distance to water. Photographs were taken and scale drawings were made of each panel of rock art. We also noted other archaeological information for each site, including lithic materials, projectile points, house rings, and ground stone.

We followed Heizer and Baumhoff's (1962:200) typology of styles, since it is widely known and provides a standardized terminology. Although critiqued by Hedges (1982), this stylistic typology remains in use, largely because no convincing alternative has been suggested to replace it, and although imperfect it is a practical classificatory system (Woody 2000a:156). We have not found pictographs of their Puebloan Painted Style in Warner Valley (not surprisingly), but all of Heizer and Baumhoff's other styles are present (table 8.1). We have found an additional style, Great Basin Carved Abstract, in Warner Valley, which is discussed below.

As we examined rock art in Warner Valley, we found that the settlement pattern model proposed by Weide (1968) was insufficient to explain the large upland sites we encountered. On the basis of elevation, we divided the 117 sites within Warner Valley into three groups. Sites with mean altitude above sea level of 1,460 meters or less were considered lowland sites; sites with elevation of 1,461 to 1,723 meters were considered to be of intermediate elevation; and sites with elevation of 1,724 meters or greater were considered upland sites. These elevations correspond with the natural terrain breaks between the basin, the intermediate territory, and the uplands. Each of the three groups contained 39 sites.

In the Warner Valley uplands, extremely large sites are more common than in the lowlands. At Long Lake, rock art covers more than 4 kilometers of rim on the west side of the lake. In 1976 the BLM discovered that an unauthorized excavation at the base of the rim had exposed a buried

TABLE 8.1 | Warner Valley Rock art Styles (Oldest Styles at the Top; Rectilinear and Curvilinear Abstract Styles Overlap and May Be Contemporaneous)

PETROGLYPHS	PICTOGRAPHS
Carved abstract	Rectilinear abstract
Pit and groove	Curvilinear abstract
Rectilinear abstract	Representational
Curvilinear abstract	
Representational	

(Cannon and Ricks 1986; Ricks and Cannon 1993)

panel of rock art (figure 8.1). This art is deeply carved into the surface of the rock, and no open space has been left within the design (figures 8.2 and 8.3). The design elements include straight lines, sinuous lines, and dots. The carved lines and dots are as much as 1.5 centimeters deep. We believe that this art merits a separate style name and have called it the Great Basin Carved Abstract (GBCA).

The BLM chose to mitigate the damage caused by the unauthorized excavation by squaring up the hole, marking the corners, and reburying the petroglyphs to the previous ground level. In doing this, the BLM found that the rock art extended approximately 1.1 meters below the surrounding ground level. Approximately 20 centimeters above the bottom of the excavation, this panel of rock art is sealed by a layer of volcanic ash approximately 10 centimeters in thickness. The ash was analyzed at Washington State University and was identified as a primary deposition from the climactic eruption of Mount Mazama, in approximately 6800 B.P. (Foit 1985). A small hearth near the top of the excavation yielded a ^{14}C date of 2160 B.P. (WSU 3364; wood charcoal). A leaf-shaped projectile point and a Northern Side-notch projectile point were found in situ in the excavation wall, as were three portable metates and a mano. One metate lay above the Mazama ash, one rested partially within the ash layer, and one was below it. The mano was slightly above the ash layer.

Limited test probes on the rim above the buried panel gave evidence of occupation before the Mazama eruptions, immediately after the eruptions, and continuing to the present. As we continued work at this site, several other panels of rock art of similar style were found in unburied contexts. These panels were severely weathered and had completely repatinated.

They were discovered by using polarized lenses at a time in the day when the angle of the sun cast raking light across rock faces. As survey continued in the area, we began to find more of these petroglyphs. We have now observed similar petroglyphs at a number of sites stretching from Warner Valley in Oregon through northern Nevada, which leads us to conclude that the GBCA rock art is more widespread than we had earlier believed. Art similar to the Great Basin Carved Abstract style has been reported from the area of Winnemucca Lake, Nevada (Connick and Connick 1995) and from Massacre Lake, Nevada (Woody 1997a). We should note that the depth of the carvings at Winnemucca Lake may, in part, be attributable to the ease of carving the tufa surfaces present there as opposed to the basalt that was used at sites with GBCA rock art north of Winnemucca Lake.

The GBCA rock art that we have found on basalt surfaces always appears to be of substantial age. The buried panel at Long Lake is at least 6,800 years old. We know this because it was sealed by volcanic ash. The ash,

Figure 8.1. South portion (Panel A) of buried rock art panel, Long Lake, Oregon. Photograph by: W. J. Cannon

however, gives us only a date after which the art could not have been made; it may be significantly older.

In addition to recording more than 20,000 individual design elements at the Long Lake site, we recorded other types of artifacts and features that were present, such as projectile points, lithic scatters, stone rings, and milling stones. More than seventy milling stones are easily visible in the area in front of the rim. These include individual portable metates, single bedrock metates, and multiple groups of bedrock metates. Numerous manos are also present. Paiute consultants have told us that when women today gather and process fruit, roots, seeds, or berries at upland sites they turn over their portable metates before leaving the site. We suspect that there may be a substantially larger number of portable milling stones on the site than we have found so far.

Although there are a number of historic petroglyphs in the area, present-day Paiute deny making them. Among the historic petroglyphs are human figures dressed in boots and wearing ten-gallon hats similar to

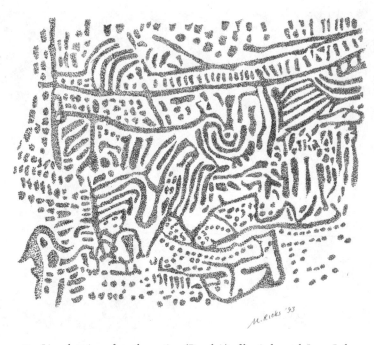

Figure 8.2. Line drawing of south portion (Panel A) of buried panel, Long Lake, Oregon. Drawing by M. Ricks

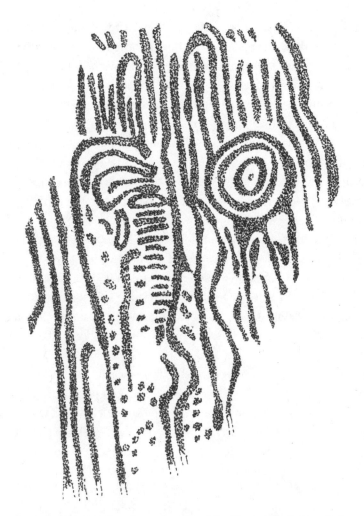

Figure 8.3. Line drawing of north portion (Panel B) of buried panel, Long Lake, Oregon. Drawing by M. Ricks

those worn by buckaroos today. There are also petroglyphs that appear to be cattle brands. Some of these may have been produced by settlers in the area; others may have been produced by Native Americans.

The ethnographic information for the Paiute in the Warner Valley and its surroundings gives little evidence about rock art. Present-day Paiute, and those who were consulted by ethnographers in the 1930s through the 1950s, deny having made it; they also deny knowledge of who made it or attribute it to supernatural beings. We are left with questions: Did the Paiute know about the rock art but choose not to share information with ethnographers? Were the historic images made by ranch hands or troops in imitation of other images they had seen on the rocks? Was there a cultural discontinuity between people who had made the rock art and those who later spoke with ethnographers?

Because we cannot answer these questions, we have chosen to examine some of the multiple contexts in which the rock art is found. This exercise helps us to better understand what was taking place where rock art was made. One problem is that which Cressman (1937:11) first highlighted: the temporal correlation of rock art with its associated contexts. As Pendegraft (chapter 5, this volume) points out, there has been a tendency for direct associations between rock art and settlement archaeology to be explained away, when not simply ignored, usually by arguing that rock art and settlement belong to different periods. Although in most cases the temporal relationship between rock art and associated archaeology is speculative, because monuments are often re-used and invested with new meanings (Bradley 1993, 2000), and because Great Basin rock art (including that in our study area) is predominantly located in the settled landscape or at places visited in the course of economic activities, it is likely that rock art was encountered regularly in domestic life and would have provoked some sort of cultural response and have been incorporated into cultural practice (Quinlan and Woody 2003:375–76). Consequently, considering rock art and physically nearby archaeological materials together represents an acknowledgment that site context is potentially an extension of site meaning (see also Pendegraft [chapter 5] and Shock [chapter 6], this volume).

Site Size

In Warner Valley occasional small isolated rock art sites with only a few pictographs or petroglyphs can be found at all elevations—lowland, intermediate, and upland. The most spectacular concentrations of rock occur in two kinds of settings. First, concentrations are found in lowland areas on lakeshores, at sites that are believed to have served as winter camps. There are several of these on the valley floor. The rock art is on large boulders, shows little repatination, and is largely representational.

The major sites, in terms of number of designs, complexity of designs, and site size, occur in the uplands, along basalt rims of sink lakes, which may be up to three miles in length. The designs appear to have been made over a long period of time, with some showing minimal repatination and others showing complete repatination.

Association of Rock Art with Food Resources—Plants

The presence of milling stones indicates that the upland area was used for the preparation of plant foods, rather than for hunting only. More than half of the rock art sites we have recorded are occupation sites. It is at these occupation sites that the largest concentrations of rock art are found. The rock art is directly within the occupation area. In many cases, stone house rings are built against a wall of the rim that is covered with rock art. Large boulders with rock art on their sides and surfaces also have from one to as many as thirteen bedrock metates present, allowing us to speculate that they functioned as community food-processing areas.

Given the plants now present in the upland areas, the sites were probably used in the late spring for processing of roots and in the summer for the processing of fruits. According to one BLM botanist, the stand of biscuit-root (*Lomatium* spp.) just south of the Long Lake site is the largest in the region. It would have provided ample opportunity to gather roots to use fresh or to dry for winter storage. In addition to the *Lomatium,* the region contains wild onions (*Allium* spp.), wild carrots or yampa (*Perideridia* spp.), and sego lily (*Calochortus macrocarpus*). Many other food plants including currants (*Ribes aureum* and *Ribes cereum*), chokecherry (*Prunus virginiana*), and Klamath plum (*Prunus subcordata*) occur in the uplands.

Because of the shallow soils in the uplands surrounding Warner Valley, test excavations have for the most part yielded little useful information. One exception is at Long Lake, where limited excavations have shown occupation of the site from the present to as far back as 7000 B.P.

Warner Valley and its uplands were divided into twenty study units, each 58 square kilometers in area (Ricks 1995:135). In addition, the three elevation zones defined—lowland, intermediate, and upland—correspond to the valley floor, the transitional zone, and the higher elevations of our study area.

Each study unit was assigned a probable vegetation type using BLM planning maps of vegetation cover (USDI Bureau of Land Management 1981). Statistical analyses (Ricks 1995:139) showed that in the uplands, rock art was most likely to be present in areas with low sage (*Artemesia arbuscula*) vegetation communities, which included plants that were economically important to the Northern Paiute at the time of Euro-American contact, such as biscuit-root (*Lomatium* spp.), bitterroot (*Lewisia rediviva*), and yampa (*Perideridia* spp.). These plant communities have probably changed little over the past several thousand years, since they grow in shallow, stony soil to which few other native plants are adapted.

In the lowlands (Ricks 1995:141) rock art is most strongly associated with big sage/bunchgrass plant communities, which include many of the plants the Northern Paiute harvested for their seeds, including Great Basin wild rye (*Elymus cinereus*), rice grass (*Oryzopsis hymenoides*), and squirreltail (*Sitanion* spp.).

Association of Rock Art with Food Resources—Animals

Although both antelope and deer are present in the upland area, hunters would probably not have had much success in the broad open area near the largest rock art sites. The noise and activity within the sites when they were occupied would probably have caused the deer to graze elsewhere. Deer in the uplands are more likely to graze singly, in areas that have some cover of brush. A hunter would have to approach with extreme caution so as not to alarm the deer before he was close enough to kill it. Antelope tend to graze in the open and in groups, which might make it possible for groups of hunters to drive them to draws or canyons, where they could be ambushed. Maps produced by the BLM (1981) provide information about current critical habitat for mule deer (*Odocoileus hemionus*), bighorn sheep (*Ovis canadensis*), antelope (*Antilocapra americana*), and sage grouse (*Centrocercus urophasianus*) on BLM holdings. The distribution of these animals across the landscape has certainly been changed by Euro-American agriculture, but we believe critical habitats may be a key to distribution in the past. The relationship between antelope habitat (Ricks 1995:145) and rock art is negative at low and intermediate elevations. In other words, rock art is less likely to be located in critical antelope habitat than in areas that are not critical habitat for antelope. The relationship between mule deer habitat and rock art is weak and negative at low elevations. At intermediate and high elevations there is no significant association. There is no statistically significant correlation between distribution of rock art sites and critical habitat for bighorn sheep at any elevation. There was no relationship between the number of sage grouse leks (strutting grounds) in a study unit and the presence of rock art at low or upland elevations. At intermediate elevations the relationship was of moderate strength and negative.

Despite the fact that rabbit bones are very common in archaeological sites throughout Warner Valley, no images of rabbits appear in the corpus of Warner Valley rock art. Waterfowl and fish bones also are common in archaeological sites in the valley, but waterfowl and fish do not appear in rock art. Further, in study units designated by BLM as bighorn sheep habitat, there are no petroglyphs of bighorn sheep, although 229 sheep images have been found in other parts of Warner Valley. These data suggest that the premise that Heizer and Baumhoff (1959, 1962) proposed does not hold true in Warner Valley. Rock art does not seem to be associated with hunting sites or with game trails.

Repatination as a Time Marker

In addition to the volcanic tephra, there were other indicators of age. Except for the buried panel, the GBCA rock art has completely repatinated so that it is indistinguishable in color from the rock surface. In many cases GBCA rock art in aboveground locations is so weathered that the designs are hard to see. Wherever the GBCA rock art occurs in association with other rock art styles common to the Warner Valley, the GBCA style always underlies all other styles. In addition to repatination of rock art, we have noted repatination of bedrock metate surfaces. Some are completely repatinated and associated with GBCA rock art. These surfaces are too frequent and much too large to have been used to grind pigment for use in pictograph manufacture. The metates are associated with occupation sites; we believe that they indicate the processing of plants at these sites over the last 10,000 years.

Associated Artifacts

Soil formation takes place very slowly in this portion of the northern Great Basin. Areas such as these upland lake playas deflate in the dry season. Therefore, few of the upland lake basins have sufficient soil to provide good stratigraphic contexts. While test excavations have yielded little stratigraphic information, projectile points from surface collections in upland sites (primarily Stemmed, Humboldt, Northern Side-notch, and Elko series) indicate that there has been nearly constant occupation throughout at least the last 7,000 years.

Superposition of Rock Art as a Time Marker

It may be, however, that the best stratigraphy is that of the art itself. In many rock art panels in the area it is possible to find superimposed three distinct ages of rock art. The degree of repatination is different for each style of art. On the basis of the degree of repatination of the art, we believe the rock art in Warner Valley falls into three chronological periods. The earliest style is the Great Basin Carved Abstract, with a minimum age of 7,000 years at the Long Lake site. This style is heavily weathered and completely repatinated where it is above the ground surface. In several areas it has been found in buried contexts. Woody (1997a) describes somewhat similar petroglyphs from Massacre Lake in northern Nevada (see also Ritter, Woody, and Watchman [chapter 9], this volume).

Great Basin Curvilinear Abstract and Rectilinear Abstract rock art appears to be intermediate in date. In most of the sites in which they are found, these styles have at least partially repatinated.

The most recent rock art is primarily of the Great Basin Representational style. This art has very little, if any, repatination present. These changes in rock art may reflect changes in the population of the region over time. The representational rock art may have flourished after the Numic expansion approximately 1,500 years ago. The changes from GBCA to other abstract styles may correspond with the Altithermal period, when warmer temperatures may have caused population movements within the region.

Association of Rock Art with Occupation Sites

As we continued to record rock art sites, it became obvious to us that we were seeing more art in residential sites than in non-residential areas. We began to think about what archaeological indicators were found within the region that are indicators of residential use. Six factors found in residential areas were not generally found in non-residential areas:

a. Stone rings (house rings)

b. Ground stones (manos, metates, mortars, pestles)

c. Midden deposits

d. Lithic scatters

e. Location in a sheltered area with important food resources nearby

f. Tools such as drills and scrapers, which are more likely to be used in "homes" than "on the road"

If a site contained at least three of these indicators, we considered it to be an occupation site.

In Warner Valley, and in the uplands surrounding it, rock art is closely associated with occupation sites. Pictographs and petroglyphs are found on the rock circles that outline house sites, within the houses, in rock shelters that appear to have been occupied, and on milling stones. Essentially, the art is in the kitchens and living rooms (see also Cannon and Woody [chapter 4], Pendegraft [chapter 5], and Shock [chapter 6], this volume).

Site Size

The number of design elements at rock art sites in Warner Valley varies widely. Some small shelters have only one or two petroglyphs or pictographs; other sites, particularly in the uplands, have more than 20,000 glyphs. In addition to rock art, we have searched for other archaeological features at these sites. We have found many metates, and examination of them shows that they, like the rock art, show degrees of repatination ranging from no patina to complete repatination. Where we find Great Basin Carved Abstract rock art, in most cases, completely repatinated grinding surfaces are also present. We believe that this common feature reflects a long-standing use of the upland areas for plant gathering and that rock art was important to the people who used the Warner Valley and its uplands over the last 10,000 years.

Taçon and Chippindale (1998) delineate the differences between informed methodology and formal methodology in the study of rock art. Informed methods "depend on some source of insight passed on directly by or indirectly from those who made and used the rock-art" (1998:6),

while formal methods "depend on no inside knowledge.... The information available is then restricted to that which is immanent in the images
themselves, or which we can discern from their relations to each other
and to the landscape, or by relation to whatever archaeological context
is available" (1998:8).

Since we have no ethnographic information that will help us to understand how people lived in the Warner Valley before the arrival of Numic-
speakers, we have largely been confined to formal methods of study. We
have examined the multiple contexts in which rock art occurs in sites in
Warner Valley in the hope of expanding our knowledge of the activities
taking place.

None of the currently proposed models for rock art seem to provide a
single overarching reason for the presence of rock art in the archaeological record for the Warner Valley. The art has been created over a period
of at least 7,000 years. Ethnographic evidence from recent and current
Northern Paiute sources provides few clues to help us to understand the
most recent of the art. There is no ethnographic information about the
pre-Paiute inhabitants of the Warner Valley that can help to explain the
art. The rock art sites do not seem to be related to hunting. They do not
appear to have any relationship to solar events or calendars. We have no
evidence to suggest that the art was made by male shamans involved in
secret and mystical activities—in fact, the location of the rock art suggests that it was within homes, in kitchens, and closely associated with
food processing. The largest and most complex rock art sites were associated with areas where plant foods were processed during the spring
and summer.

Rock art is also found at lowland sites that served as winter camps. The
art in these lowland sites is largely representational and tends to occur on
boulders rather than on rims. It also is found in locations that would be
clearly visible to all the group members.

We believe that rock art may have served a function related to social
solidarity within the culture of the groups that assembled in winter to
camp along lowland lakeshores and in the spring and summer in upland
sites to harvest vegetable foods and hunt. Since the art occurs in public
contexts, and often within the contexts of homes or shelters, we believe

that it was meant for the entire group and that the creating of rock art was participatory rather than exclusionary. It may have had an instructional function, serving to reinforce core values. As our work to record new sites continues, we hope to discover more about the place of rock art in the lives of the ancient inhabitants of the Warner Valley.

CHAPTER 9

Petroglyph Dating on the Massacre Bench

ERIC W. RITTER, ALANAH WOODY, AND

ALAN WATCHMAN

While many archaeologists show great interest in rock art, direct dating remains critical to the integration of rock art research into mainstream archaeology. When the production of rock art can be situated in time, it can be analyzed alongside other concurrent cultural practices and a more richly textured study of prehistoric human behavior developed. Only when rock art can be placed within its larger social context can it be reasonably understood as a part of the complex lifeways of indigenous peoples.

This comprehension is, however, not necessarily the case in analyzing the *use* of rock art, since these sites appear in many cases to have been utilized over very long periods of time. Once a monument (like rock art) becomes a part of the landscape, it begins to influence later inhabitants, perhaps even drawing people to it (Bradley 1993:2, 5–6, 1997:11, 1998). These places probably accumulated meanings through time and came to be perceived as places where ancestors had left their mark (i.e., rock art), thereby becoming points of articulation between time and space through re-use (Basso 1996:62; Bradley 1993:53). In this way rock art may have been instrumental in the shaping of social relationships through reference to the past and the place as a part of the cultural landscape created by the ancestors for subsequent use by their descendants (Taçon 1994:118; Woody 2000a:231).

Although the use-life of rock art extends beyond its actual production, and possibly even into the present, the importance of identifying its starting point is not diminished. Establishing the point in time at which rock art enters into, or begins to help shape, the cultural landscape, allows for clarifying the possible sequence of use and articulation with associated behaviors. Direct dating of rock art does not answer all—or arguably even the most important—questions, but it does provide a significant starting point for analysis.

In the past, without reliable methods of direct dating, several approaches have been used in estimating the age of rock art. Identification of datable objects or animals in the imagery as a means of determining age of rock art is problematic at best (Bednarik 2001; Tuohy 1969), but it has proven useful in some cases (Grant, Baird, and Pringle 1968). Although traditional relative dating methods such as superposition, seriation, and analysis of differential patination can also be useful (Chippindale and Taçon 1998; Lee and Hyder 1990; Loendorf 1994), such methods are not without their critics (Bednarik 2002; Dorn 1998a:69–96; Whitley et al. 1984). Bettinger and Baumhoff (1982) used differences in petroglyph manufacture as one factor in hypothesizing the expansion of populations who spoke a Numic language into the Great Basin and thus dating "styles" of Great Basin rock art, although this approach has been contested (Ritter 1994). It remains difficult at best, however, to unambiguously relate rock art manufacture to other site activities without direct, reliable dating.

Pictograph dating is generally well accepted, simply because the binders used to produce paint are often organic and so accelerator mass spectrometry radiocarbon ($AMS^{14}C$) and other traditional dating techniques work reliably and are widely used (Chaffee, Hyman, and Rowe 1993a, 1993b; Clottes 1998a; Watchman 1993b).

Petroglyph varnish dating using cation-ratio techniques showed early promise (Dorn 1983; Dorn and Whitley 1984), but controversy arose (Bierman and Gillespie 1991; Bierman, Gillespie, and Kuehner 1991; Dorn 1994a, 1997; Harry 1995; Watchman 1992, 1993a) and the method has since been abandoned by its developer (Dorn 1996). However, some researchers continue to use it (Tratebas 1999), in an apparent effort to refine the technique. Methods of AMS ^{14}C dating of petroglyph varnish have also been developed (Dorn 1998b; Watchman 1999; Watchman et al. 1993), and in this chapter we present the results of one such study on petroglyphs on the Massacre Bench in northwestern Nevada. The limitations of varnish and other rock art dating techniques have been discussed by Bednarik (2002), but in general, limitations revolve around the great likelihood of contamination of samples, the fact that "dates" obtained are actually only broad ranges of time, and basic flaws in the assumptions upon which interpretations are made.

MASSACRE BENCH ENVIRONMENT

At the northwestern corner of the Basin and Range physiographic province near the intersection of the Nevada, California, and Oregon borders lies the volcanic tableland or plateau of the Silver State's Massacre Bench (see figure 1.1). Within this bench are numerous petroglyph locations, three of which form the focus of this discussion. Occurring throughout the region are numerous sources of obsidian and cryptocrystalline silicate materials that served as tool stone, generally in dispersed cobble and pebble form (Hughes 1986).

The Massacre Bench (ca. 4,400 hectares) was formed by uplifting of the underlying basaltic cap to a maximum elevation of about 2,000 meters, which drops abruptly over 300 meters to the west into Long Valley. The bench slopes gently to the east and southeast, to the Massacre Lakes playa system at an elevation of 1,712 meters and farther east to the Bitner Table (2,000 meters elevation). To the north of the Massacre Bench are Bald Mountain Canyon, Sheldon Antelope Refuge, and, farther to the north, the Coleman and Warner valleys, all major locations of largely similar rock art. While the Massacre Bench itself is defined by major rimrocks (5–10 meters high or more) on the west and south especially, within the bench are many smaller (1–5 meters high) rimrocks, taluses, and boulder clusters that include the dominant petroglyph sites.

Soils and vegetation within the Massacre Bench are well-drained, very cobbly loams to extremely cobbly loams dominated by low sagebrush, bluebunch wheatgrass, Cusick bluegrass, Nevada bluegrass, and rubber rabbitbrush (sagebrush-grassland steppe). With increased elevation the western juniper belt emerges. Junipers, along with small locations of big sage, desert parsley, and wild onion, are found around the principal petroglyph sites discussed herein (Slusser 1999:31, 41). The changes in vegetation since the Euro-American entrance have been well chronicled by Raven (1981). ·

The Massacre Bench today has plentiful water sources, with a number of springs occurring not coincidentally with two of the three study sites and elsewhere scattered within the bench. Rock tanks that hold seasonal water are present in small canyons as well as several small seeps at the third site, and scattered ephemeral to intermittent drainages occur along with small seasonal playas.

While wildlife patterns have been altered by the introduction of livestock and habitat changes, pronghorn (*Antilocapra americana*) and deer (*Odocoileus hemionus*) are still common. An antelope migratory path passes close to the subject sites (Heizer and Baumhoff 1962:figure 15). Bighorn sheep probably occurred in low numbers at or near the study area. Numerous other smaller mammals frequent the locality as well.

ETHNOGRAPHIC AND ARCHAEOLOGICAL SETTING

When Euro-American interlopers began travels and explorations in this region in the 1840s, they encountered bands of Northern Paiute. While the ethnographic record is imprecise regarding which hunter-gatherer bands may have used the Massacre Bench, most likely it was the Aga ipañiñadökadö, the Fish Lake Eaters or Fish Eaters or the Moadökadö, the Wild Onion Eaters (Stewart 1939:135–36). ·

The length of regional occupation and use of the area by Northern Paiute is problematic. Excavations by Layton in rock shelters near the Massacre Bench led him to conclude that "climatically induced environmental changes may have forced pre-Numic abandonment of areas later settled by Numic populations" (T. N. Layton 1985:195). Linguistic analysis of place names and borrowings from Sahaptian suggests a recent arrival of the Northern Paiute in the northern Great Basin (Foster 1996:94). Nearby Surprise Valley to the west may have been abandoned until well into the nineteenth century, perhaps because the valley "marked the unfriendly boundary between newly arrived Paiute in the High Rock country to the east and Pit River peoples to the west" (T. N. Layton 1985:197). Kelly (1932:72) believed Klamath ancestors were the previous occupants of Surprise Valley and were perhaps driven out.

The earliest archaeological work in the Massacre locality was the description of amateur collections of prehistoric materials from Massacre Lake Cave (Heizer 1942), work amplified later by Ritter (1966). This large cave exhibited many perishables and is multi-component, but lacks rock art, despite suitable surfaces. Heizer found the assemblages to be "most closely related to those of south-central Oregon, yet at the same time certain features are reminiscent of types from the Nevada caves to the south" (1942:123). Pacific shell artifacts suggest contact to the west and northwest.

Since Heizer's early study, the northwest corner of Nevada and overlapping areas of California and Oregon have not been ignored archaeologically. On the basis of extensive archaeological work within and around the Massacre Bench, Leach (1988:93) has defined a four-period cultural chronology for the locality. The earliest period—9000–4500 B.C.—is labeled the Pre-Archaic. This period is followed by the Early Archaic (4500–1000 B.C.), the Middle Archaic (1000 B.C.–A.D. 500), and the Late Archaic (A.D. 500–1850). While there is some variation in the timing of each period, Leach's sequence closely matches those for the neighboring Surprise Valley (O'Connell 1971, 1975) and for the High Rock country to the south (Layton 1970). However, on the basis of archaeological constructs, settlement and resource use patterns are not exactly equivalent (cf. Leach 1988:206).

It has been suggested that in the Massacre Bench locality from Early Archaic times until contact, intensification of settlement activity occurred in nearly all ecozones, from wetlands and marshes of the Massacre Lakes to upland areas, in an attempt to increase food output for a growing population (Leach 1988:203–4). Leach hypothesizes that the greatest occupation density and resource competition occurred during the Middle and Late Archaic, with the most obvious signs of subsistence intensification and diversification (1988:204). Perhaps most relevant to regional rock art studies is Leach's finding that Late Archaic populations focused their efforts in the uplands and near springs, and in different ecozones than in earlier periods. Woody (1997a:54) believes the settlement-subsistence and demographic change during Middle and Late Archaic times is reflected in the rock art of one of the major upland petroglyph sites (26WA78, also listed as 26WA69 in earlier works) studied here.

REGIONAL ROCK ART

Rock art studies in the Massacre Bench locality and adjoining regions have a long history, beginning with documentation of sites in the 1950s by Dale Ritter (Ritter 1961, 1965). Heizer and Baumhoff (1962) used some of this documentation in their seminal volume on Great Basin rock art, and all posited a relationship of the rock art with hunting magic. A hiatus of sorts existed in the regional rock art studies until Leach's (1988) spatial analysis of settlement structure. In terms of prehistoric sites, rock art locales are a minor component, with sixteen known sites of variable size (all within the bench area at a density of about one per 2,750 hectares. Leach states: "Rock art sites often appear in settings similar to upland temporary camps or hunting stations, particularly where water occurs. Canyon rims or isolated basalt boulders, often in drainages, near springs, or at overlooks above game trails are frequent locales. Simple to complex abstract and geometric designs, either pecked or scratched into the patinated surfaces or basalt boulders, can cover single or many hundreds of panels" (1988:46).

Two of the authors (Ritter and Woody) have been attracted to the outstanding research opportunities in rock art studies offered by the shelter and open rock art of the region, and their work has resulted in a number of reports and publications, of which this chapter is a continuation (Ritter 1994, 2002; Woody 1997a). This work, in turn, has been complemented by rock art studies just to the north in Oregon, particularly in the Warner Valley (Cannon and Ricks 1986; Ricks 1995; Ricks and Cannon 1993; Ross 2000; and see Boreson [chapter 7], Cannon and Woody [chapter 4], Cannon and Ricks [chapter 8], and Shock [chapter 6], this volume).

The search for earlier episodes of rock art manufacture is a central focus for this study and has been an orientation of earlier works by Cannon, Ricks, and Woody. Of particular interest here, Cannon and Ricks (1986; Ricks and Cannon 1993) have defined a Great Basin Carved Abstract style (see figures 8.2 and 8.3). One panel of this style in the vicinity of the Warner Valley was covered with Mount Mazama ash dated about 6,800 years ago. It is clearly among the oldest in the northern Great Basin. It is this presumed style and its dating that are the principal focus of this paper.

Woody's study of the main Massacre Bench site (26WA78) led to the definition of four rock art generations proposed to run from 11,000 years ago to less than 1,500 years ago (1997a:182). Projectile point forms found at this rock art site and others on the Massacre Bench are similar in age range, including a crescent, Great Basin Stemmed points, and later types. Woody (1997a:180) hypothesizes that the increase in rock art production of the Middle Archaic (generations 2 and 3) is in agreement with Leach's (1988) change in resource intensification at about the same time.

Ritter (1994) has studied the locality's scratched rock art, concluding that it is long-lived, often integral to pecked designs, and possibly related to women's activities and shamanistic power/place associations.

THE STUDY SITES

Three petroglyph sites on the Massacre Bench were selected for varnish sampling in an attempt to establish a chronological context for the region's older-appearing rock art. Panels were preselected in 2000 based on subjective evaluations of style and level of weathering and rock coating. One of the three sites under current laboratory constraints provided dates discussed below. Each of the sampled sites is characterized briefly below.

Massacre Lake Site (26WA78)

This site was formerly published under the University of California Berkeley number 26WA69 by Heizer and Baumhoff (1962:65–67) and is by far the most extensive petroglyph site in the region. Designated the Massacre Lake Site, it is actually situated on the Massacre Bench less than 10 kilometers to the north of the major playa system. This rock art site with adjoining extensive lithic scatter (Ricks 1998) extends for about 3 kilometers along a generally easterly facing rimrock punctuated by several small canyons with seasonal water tanks and at least one seep. Rock enclosures occur sporadically on the rimrock. The site contains more than 500 panels of single and multiple motifs numbering in the thousands, many superimposed (see Woody 1997a). An assessment of the most weathered figures of the presumed Great Basin Carved Abstract style suggests a minimum of 25 panels (4 percent of those present). In this locality the petroglyphs associated with this style are from 2 to 5 millimeters deep, with lines 8 to 30 millimeters wide. Most of these older-appearing weathered glyphs are patinated to a dark brown oxidized surface and fail to exhibit extensive varnish formation. Varnish samples were obtained by the authors from one of the "oldest style" panels (Panel 16) within deep, broadly grooved grid and caternary curve motifs, as well as from nearby natural varnish surfaces. This panel provided the dating discussed below. Overall, the petroglyphs were 2.5YR 3/2 (dusky red) on a rock with background colors of 5YR 3/1 (very dark gray) and 5YR 5/2 (reddish gray), using Munsell Rock Color descriptions. Black varnish occurs both within the grooves and on the rock surface.

Sage Hen Springs (26wa6916)

This 0.5-kilometer-long petroglyph site is located approximately 1 kilometer north of the main Massacre site discussed above. It also lies along an easterly facing rimrock adjoining a spring complex. A temporary prehistoric camp, with possible subsurface deposits, adjoins the site. A small tuffaceous tubular pipe was found at the base of one panel. There are approximately 281 panels of petroglyphs at this site similar to the site described above. At least 18 (6 percent) of the panels exhibit deeply weathered and partially varnished petroglyphs similar to the Great Basin Carved Abstract style. Munsell readings of the sampled petroglyphs (Panel 78) are 5YR 3/3 (dark reddish brown) with the background rock 5YR 3/2 (dark reddish brown). Such color readings do not include the black small patches of varnish within certain petroglyph elements. Varnish samples were secured from three panels. Panel 65 includes three vertical rows of cupules, or deep dots. Panel 78 includes a sequence of long, slightly curving, generally parallel grooves. Panel 100 includes a grid-like motif, also with a dark reddish brown color mixed with black varnish patches within the grooves. A nearby unmarked varnished rimrock face was also sampled.

Tuffy Springs (26wa2456)

This site along a low, generally east-facing rimrock more than 1 kilometer in length contains 118 panels, of which 21 percent (25) are older, varnished or heavily weathered petroglyphs of the presumed Great Basin Carved Abstract style. A spring occurs just below the rock-art-covered escarpment, and numerous flaked and ground stone artifacts and bedrock milling slicks were observed at the presumed residential base. One rock enclosure is also located adjoining the petroglyphs. Panel 45 was sampled from this site, a complex panel with older petroglyphs that include grid-like images, curved parallel lines, parallel line sequences along rock edges, and a single pole ladder-like design. More recent figures include several lizard-like designs. The older petroglyphs are a 10YR 3/1 color, dark reddish gray, which is the same as the background rock color. Within some of the grooves are extensive concentrations of black varnish. Background varnish samples were also taken on undecorated portions of the main face.

With regard to the sampled grooves and cupules, these were generally not smooth, and black lichens are apparent in some of the older-appearing grooves. In some of the ancient-appearing petroglyphs it is possible that an older, slick black manganese-like skin may have weathered away in part or totally. It is also clear that sloping surfaces with deeper, wider older-style grooves or cupules tend to have more varnish as a result of their trapping effects for water, dust, and airborne organic particles, and microenvironments conducive to organic growth. Thus, as is commonly known, the degree of varnish presence, and especially color (Whitley et al. 1984), is not necessarily a measure of antiquity.

Sampling Methods

Rock varnish samples were collected from two off-art locations and from a carved line on Panel 16 at the Massacre Lake site (26WA78). The rock art is situated on a sloping surface of basalt measuring approximately 90 by 120 centimeters. The relative thickness and general appearance of the varnishes indicate that the carving has weathered to an intermediate state between that on the broken surface near the carving and the darker off-art sample. The carving that was sampled (the inner grooved line) is part of a series of curved grooves or arcs that run upward from the broken lower part of the panel and then bend over in a broad curve.

Samples of varnish were progressively removed from the three surfaces by first cleaning with a brush and then systematically excavating the dark coating with an Arlec engraving tool powered by a battery and fitted with a dental burr. Powdered varnish was brushed from the micro-excavations onto aluminum foil, which was folded, labeled, and stored. The brown varnish from the broken lower edge was removed in two stages: an upper layer and the varnish formed directly on the basalt (16A). The lower sample was submitted for radiocarbon analysis. For the carved groove, the brown-black varnish in small depressions within the groove was targeted. The surface layer of each depression was lightly excavated and discarded, and the second layer was removed to the bedrock and retained for dating (16B). Three dark brown-black rocks adjacent to the panel were collected as off-art samples, and the basal layer of varnish from one rock (16R) was used for dating. The other scraped samples were retained for geochemical analyses.

The purpose of scraping the basal layer of varnish from each location was to determine when the varnish started to form. For the darkest off-art sample, the age estimate of varnish formation likely indicated a maximum age for the carvings. The geological sample of varnish from the broken ledge was not as dark and was thinner than varnish in the grooves, and it was considered in the field that the age of formation of this varnish should be younger than the varnish in the groove. This subjective assessment was based on previous experience in collecting and dating rock varnishes. The age estimate for the geological varnish should support the field observation, on the one hand, and on the other, it should provide a guide as to the reliability of the AMS ^{14}C dating method for this panel. If the age for varnish on this broken surface was older than for varnish in the groove or the darker varnish (off-art), then the dating result would be regarded as unacceptable. In summary, the expectation in the field was that the age of the varnish from the base of the coating in the carved groove would be younger than the darkest off-art sample and older than the lighter varnish from the broken edge.

Analytical Results

The samples were sent for radiocarbon assay to the National Ocean Sciences Accelerator Mass Spectrometry Facility at Woods Hole, Massachusetts. At this laboratory the rock varnish was subjected to oxidation of the contained organic components followed by graphitization of the evolved carbon dioxide gas (Currie et al. 2000; Gagnon et al. 2000). The graphite produced from these preparation procedures was used as a target in the ion source before the accelerator mass spectrometry measurement was performed. Uncalibrated radiocarbon age determinations are listed in table 9.1. A stable carbon isotopic ratio (*^{13}C) of -24.4 percent was measured for the varnish from the carved groove (16B).

TABLE 9.1 | Summary of Sample Sizes, Locations, $AMS^{14}C$ Measurements and Calibrated Age Estimates for Organic Material at the Base of Varnish Coatings On and Near Panel 16, Massacre Lake Site (26WA78)

SAMPLE ID AND LAB. NUMBER	LOCATION OF VARNISH	VARNISH WEIGHT (GM)	RADIOCARBON AGE (YEARS BP)	CALIBRATED B.C. AGE (YEARS)
16A B os34030	Off-art lower ledge	0.11544	2560 ± 410	1211-176
16B B os34029	Carved groove	0.04570	2900 ± 550	1749-397
16R B os34072	Adjacent off-art	0.03337	5760 ± 650	5362-3960

Are the results reasonable in terms of thickness, color, situation, and archaeology? The organic components in the base layers of the varnishes are presumed to have been included in the manganese-rich rock surface coatings as they formed, and they therefore indicate minimum ages for varnish formation. Uncertainty always exists in any radiocarbon dating analysis because absolute surety about the origins of all sources of carbon is not possible. This factor, along with the isolated location of the rock surfaces on the Massacre Bench, indicates a low probability that contaminants from modern sources, particularly human interference, have affected the age determinations.

The age determinations are consistent with field observations concerning the relative ages of varnish formation at the respective sampling locations. The measured age of the varnish in the carved groove is between that of the varnishes in off-art locations, confirming the opinion that the carving was done before the lower edge broke and after varnish had commenced on adjacent rocks. While the relative age confirmation does not prove the reliability of the determinations, it increases the probability that the measurements are a good approximation of the true age of the carving. The petroglyph on Panel 16 is therefore very likely more than 2,900 years old, and possibly more than 4,000 years old, given the slow rate of varnish formation.

There is no evidence of charcoal, coal, or coal-like substances in the varnishes in the Massacre Bench area (Beck et al. 1998) that would adversely affect the dating results. Dithionite and acid dissolution of the iron-rich varnishes and manganese-rich varnishes reveals no physical contaminants in the varnish residue, only short fibrous strands and insoluble pollen-like material. This carbon-bearing material was the source of the carbon used in the AMS ^{14}C dating procedure.

The stable carbon isotope measurement indicates a source of carbon related to C3 plants (plants using the most common form of photosynthesis) and not C4 plants (arid-adapted), which might have been expected if the varnish had formed in a semiarid or arid environment. A more negative value than for the C3 pathway for incorporation of carbon in the glyph possibly indicates a slightly wetter environment than at present. Since only one measurement was made, it is difficult to emphasize this point, but nevertheless it is a guide as to the more humid environmental conditions under which the varnish formed.

These preliminary results indicate a relatively young age for the petroglyphs, younger than expected from the regional archaeology as described above, and therefore they could reflect possible young contamination. Carbon-bearing components that are younger than the engraving age may have entered the varnish during the cementing of the iron and manganese oxides and clay to form the varnish. This ongoing process adds progressively younger material to the coating as the coating increases in thickness. The micro-excavation technique was used to remove most of the surface varnish, thus minimizing the contamination from the basal layer that lay directly on the pecked or "engraved" rock. Remnant young varnish may have been present in isolated micro-topographic high spots in the sampled area, which could account for a slightly younger age. The results from the field and laboratory procedures produce a minimum-limiting age, and so the carving must be older than the age of the carbon extracted and used for dating. How much older the carving is than the varnish (or the age of the carbon in the basal varnish) is uncertain, but an assumption is that the varnishing process takes approximately 1,000 to 1,500 years to completely cover a stable rock surface. Even with this additional age limit on the varnishing process, the age is still too young, given the age expected on the basis of the archaeology. Further research is necessary to verify the outcome of the present dating analyses. A program of uranium-series dating research on rock varnishes has commenced (Australian Research Council grant to Watchman), and samples of varnish from this area will be used to determine whether uranium isotopes can provide a better way for dating petroglyphs and to validate or refute the radiocarbon age determinations from the Massacre Bench area.

Most, if not all of the Great Basin rock art chronometric studies to date must be considered initial efforts, this work notwithstanding. This chapter and an earlier related work by Watchman and Woody (2002) are pioneering attempts at dating the earlier-appearing rock art at several major Great Basin localities. The results are preliminary by any estimation.

It is likely that these petroglyphs were made during the summer, since heavy regional snows would have made access difficult. The general continuity of production at the same sites suggests long-term site utilization each summer over at least the last 3,000 years and probably much longer. In general, hunter-gatherer populations do not support specialists, but because of the considerable time and effort required to produce these panels, their presence may perhaps suggest a "rock art specialist" of some type within the group(s).

As with most analyses, more questions than answers are raised by this initial study. The approximately 2900 B.P. age estimate for the one panel glyph may only be a minimal date, as suggested. Dorn (1998b:186–247) has discussed in detail variability in rock varnish within a locality and beyond and differential preservation resulting from leaching, aeolian abrasion, and the like. He cautions that "appearance equates to age is in error" (1998b:219). Furthermore, in earlier work he discusses some of the problems found in radiocarbon dating varnish over petroglyphs (Dorn 1994a:30–32, 1994b). It is in this regard that both the age estimate and the presumed presence of the Great Basin Carved Abstract style much more recently than supposed must be open to challenge.

If, however, further studies prove the dates provided here to be reliable, is the rock art at the Massacre Lake site coincidental with a climatic change proposed by Wigand (1987) in nearby Oregon? The stable isotopic measurement, in addition, gives some credibility to this belief. If so, then is this climatic change related to the culture change proposed by Leach (1988) and supported by Woody (1997a), between the Early Archaic and the Middle/Late Archaic? There appears to be a much smaller number of panels at all three sites that look very old. If this is the case, is there a relationship to lower population density and/or rock art manufacturing events? How does the date of the rock art at the Massacre Lake site fit into the suggestion that the Great Basin Carved Abstract style may transcend the middle to lower Holocene (ca. 7000–2900 years B.P.)?

This study is very preliminary, but we believe that the methodology utilized here holds great promise. Further work is anticipated, especially on the other samples and on additional panels as dating and micro-environmental analysis methods improve. It remains critical that all due caution be taken in the evaluation of its results—this is only a stepping-stone to further refinements in rock art dating. A number of questions, both technical and procedural, remain unanswered. For example, in this study the darker varnish at Tuffy Springs (26WA2456) did not provide adequate organic materials to allow dating, even though the same weight of varnish was collected. How, then, is the selection of sampling locations to be standardized, if possible, if the visual assessment of varnish accumulation is not reliable? Additionally, the precise nature of the carbonic materials that yield dates is not clearly defined; further research is already focusing attention on this difficult problem. And finally, future analysis depends on refining techniques of collection and accelerator mass spectrometry measurements. Direct dating of rock art remains a critical goal that must be pursued on a number of fronts. Only when rock art can be situated in time and analyzed within the cultural milieu that produced it can it be reasonably understood. This study is one preliminary step in that direction.

CHAPTER 10

Rock Art as an Artifact of Religion and Ritual

The Archaeological Construction of Rock Art's Past and Present Social Contexts

ANGUS R. QUINLAN

This chapter examines why rock art researchers tend to assume that rock art is in some sense religious or ritual in its original context of use and explores how such an assumption shapes discussions about the public's appropriation of rock art imagery. Academic interpretation defines what constitutes rock art's discursive field, as well as the individuals authorized to interpret and control rock art imagery. This role of academic practice is not surprising, since in its aboriginal cultural context symbolism is frequently a source of power and the locus of disputes regarding authorized readings of it (Bourdieu 1991). Academic study of rock art helps create the conditions necessary for the commodification (or wider circulation) of rock art imagery by giving it a social and cultural resonance for Western publics who are culturally unrelated to it. By imputing a sacred quality to all rock art, and reacting against interpretations that try to demystify it by uncovering a latent social practicality to it, we run the risk of fetishizing our object of study and reinforcing public stereotypes about hunter-gatherer worldviews. Yet ascribing a sacred status to rock art does not necessarily protect rock art sites against bad archaeological practices or uninformed public visitation.

Although it now seems natural to assume that rock art is self-evidently religious and an important cultural resource, nothing in its actual character makes such assumptions inevitable. The authenticity of European cave art was tied to considerations of its antiquity. Thus, when Altamira was discovered in 1879 it was not recognized as being of any great antiquity, partly because the art was too "good" to be ancient and was considered by some to be a modern forgery. Subsequent discoveries of parietal art were also believed to be modern fakes. It was not until the 1900s when the quantity of evidence had become overwhelming that the antiquity of European cave art was finally accepted (Bahn and Vertut 1997:16–22). Recognition of the art's great antiquity allowed it to become a proper object of study, and that, because of the evolutionist approaches then current, facilitated a religious interpretation of its original cultural significance.

This scenario illustrates that one potential source of cultural value for rock art is its perceived relationship with non-Western practices and theories of being. When the authorship of European cave art was associated with modern shepherds or other cave visitors, it was disparaged as meaningless graffiti. Once it was temporally distanced from the present, however, it was interpreted as a culturally meaningful practice, in part because that distancing allowed its authorship to be attributed to the Other. Beyond Europe, rock art is valued for its connection with indigenous peoples, rather than temporally distant populations, and thus dating has little impact on cultural valuations. This probably explains why historic imagery (or Western subjects portrayed in rock art) tends not to arouse much academic comment since it is not descriptive of indigenous theories of being.

In Europe antiquity remains an importance source of valuation for rock art, as exemplified by the dating controversy surrounding the Foz Côa petroglyphs. When this body of open-air art in Portugal was threatened by the construction of a large hydroelectric dam, the main argument made to save the art was that it was Paleolithic in age. Stylistic (Clottes 1998b; Zilhão 1995) and scientific analyses (Bednarik 1995; Watchman 1995, 1997) were carried out to support the conservation campaign, but the scientific techniques concluded that the art was much more recent in age. The latter finding was described as unhelpful in the campaign to save the art from dam construction, since public support for stopping the construction of the dam fell dramatically after the "announcement of the pseudo-scientific dating results obtained by Robert G. Bednarik and Alan Watchman" (Zilhão 2003:58). Yet, if the art had value in its own right, arguments about its antiquity should have had little effect on valuations of its cultural importance and eligibility for preservation.

Since the 1900s religious interpretations of rock art have prevailed— hunting magic, totemic, and shamanistic explanations reflect changing fashions in the interpretation of ethnographic data. Yet their varying accounts of the performative aspects of rock art imagery reflect, however weakly, Western notions of the function of art as iconography. The iconoclastic movement that began in the eighth century A.D., although ultimately unsuccessful, transformed the way that Western traditions viewed art placed in religious contexts. No longer was church art viewed as an illustration for the illiterate; instead, it was seen as a mysterious reflection of the supernatural world (Gombrich 1998 [1950]:138). Our predisposition to regard rock art as religious symbolism in part reflects this heritage and leads us to forget that indigenous arts are complex and multifunctional, that meanings are fluid (Layton 1991, 1992; Sperber 1975), and that the human modifications that mark sacred places are not restricted to modes of visual expression. (It should be remembered that perhaps the majority of sacred spaces recognized by humans are "natural" places unmodified by actions or markings; see Carmichael et al. 1994).

Once the antiquity of European cave art was established, interpretation of its functions and meanings increasingly referred to magico-religious practices. Reinach (1903) proposed that cave art was embedded in hunting magic rituals, basing his argument on Spencer and Gillen's (1899) ethnographic reports from Australia. The selection of Australia as the source of ethnographic analogy was neither fortuitous nor the result of bias in the anthropological record. Evolutionist approaches that were then current believed that Australian Aborigines had the most "primitive" culture and were thus relics from humanity's distant past. Frazer (1922:63), in attempting to argue that magic evolved before religion, found that his theory was "confirmed by the observation that among the Aborigines of Australia, the rudest savages as to whom we possess accurate information, magic is universally practised, whereas religion . . . seems to be nearly unknown." Similarly, Durkheim's (1995 [1912]) inquiry to delimit the essential properties of religion concentrated on Australia, in part because of the quality of ethnographic documentation it provided, but also because "what I propose above all to study . . . is the most primitive and simplest religion that can be found. To discover that religion, therefore, it is natural for me to address myself to societies that stand as close as possible to the origins of evolution. . . . Now, there are no societies that exhibit this characteristic more fully than do the Australian tribes" (Durkheim 1995 [1912]:93).

It was therefore easy for Reinach and other interpreters of European cave art to equate the cultural practices of Paleolithic hunter-gatherers with those of the Australian Aborigines and assume a magico-religious explanation (Bahn 1991:1). Ever since, it has been widely assumed that rock art is embedded in religious institutions. The rare attempts to challenge such a position, such as theories like art for art's sake (Halverson 1987), hunting instruction (Mithen 1988), or ethnographic descriptions that some rock art was made "just for fun" (Kehoe 2000:71; Stewart 1942:321), generate criticism (Lewis-Williams and Dowson 1994:202–3). The purpose of the art cannot, it seems, be reduced to simple and basic human impulses or be found to have a latent practicality. Likewise the "meaning" of imagery must always be serious and metaphorical—for example, avian imagery in rock art is interpreted as depictions of shamanic soul flight (Hedges 1985:86–91; Schaafsma 1994:51–53; Turpin 1994:81–92), and the rock surface is viewed as a thin veil between this world and that of the supernatural (Lewis-Williams and Dowson 1990). Indeed, currently popular approaches tend to challenge researchers to ask *how* rock art is religious (more specifically, shamanic or shamanistic), not *why it might be* (Lewis-Williams 1997:323–34).

This preference for magico-religious explanations runs the risk of maintaining the myth of "primitive piety" (Douglas 1975:81), reinforcing public stereotypes about hunter-gatherer belief systems. Hunting magic theory reinforced public conceptions of hunter-gatherer life as a harsh struggle for food necessitating magical intervention, as well as providing a rich seam of humor for cartoonists (for examples, see Bahn 1991). Recent shamanistic approaches do little to challenge public stereotypes of hunter-gatherers as being predominantly mystical in outlook, as foragers are portrayed as perceiving their natural and physical landscapes in pre-dominantly "mystical" terms (Clottes and Lewis-Williams 1998:81; Lewis-Williams 1991; Ouzman 1998:331). Indeed, a resurrection of evolutionist thinking is implied in justifications of ethnographic analogy to interpret the prehistoric art of the European caves, arguing that "in all these cases we are dealing with the same human species at the same degree of eco-nomic evolution, which implies affinities in behaviour, beliefs and modes of thought" (Clottes and Lewis-Williams 1998:63).

Perhaps one reason that the circulation of rock art imagery in public media has proved unsettling to a number of researchers has to do with this preference for magico-religious explanations. All archaeologists feel revulsion about artifacts circulating as commodities. However, rock art imagery usually circulates not as the object itself but as a representation of the object. The circulation of rock art imagery on media as diverse as mugs, ties, T-shirts, badges, and so on, has led to some soul-searching. Hyder (1999:vii) asks: "Are we appropriating the imagery of another cul-ture for our own commercial gain and thereby destroying its value? Do our actions honor or violate the intentions of the artists whose work we copy and mass produce?" This issue is particularly acute in areas where indigenous communities do not directly control the circulation of rock art imagery, and it contrasts strongly with Western Australia, where it is an offense to take a photograph of rock art for publication without the permission of the traditional custodians (Bednarik 2001:83).

In general, we recognize two broad kinds of appropriation of rock art imagery—its use as decoration and its use by contemporary artists (Dow-son 1999:3). Although here I focus on the former appropriation of rock art imagery, this is not to imply that the uses made of rock art by con-temporary artists are without problems. However, the legitimacy of con-temporary artistic use of imagery provides an example of archaeologists' asserting their perceived rights to control access to rock art by recognizing selected artists as having acquired the right to exploit rock art in their artworks (Dowson 1999).

The use of rock art as decoration in popular material culture is regarded as problematic because imagery is reproduced without regard to its integ-rity or accuracy. Empirically unfaithful copies are argued to entirely destroy the image's original meaning and represent the worst kind of appropriation: "Insensitively and unfaithfully re-produced images merely legitimate the simplistic and often racist attitudes people have about rock art and its producers" (Dowson 1999:5).

Further, the images selected for circulation in public media are often unrepresentative of a body of rock art and help to foster a misleading picture of the art. Dowson (1999:6) notes that in South Africa there is strong preference for the reproduction of hunting scenes, a preference that helps support popular "misconceptions" that the art is associated with hunting magic and that it depicts aspects of everyday life. (These popular "misconceptions" are theories to which Dowson is not personally sympathetic; a more balanced criticism would be that the public is not subjected to a representative range of current theories of rock art interpretation).

In the Great Basin the preference is for elaborate anthropomorphs and bighorn sheep, thus elevating these naturalistic forms above more-common and more-characteristic abstract forms. As Woody (2000a:157–58) notes, it should be borne in mind that the reproduction of naturalistic forms is in part the result of the cognitive dissonance experienced when engaging with abstract forms that are hard to classify and re-identify. Further, the images selected for publication in academic media are often unavoidably unrepresentative and selective, which Dowson is no doubt aware of, having been criticized (with Lewis-Williams) for selectively omitting figures from some of their illustrations (Skotnes 1991). (An academic paper on anthropomorph forms, for example, will, not surprisingly, reproduce mainly anthropomorph forms to support and illustrate its discussion. Selective reproduction of imagery becomes a problem with reports that are intended as a total documentation of the features and attributes of a rock art site but reproduce only an unrepresentative sample of imagery, or record only motif types that have resonance for the contemporary observer; see Woody [2000a] for further discussion).

Commodification is usually understood in the sense of economic valuation; however, rock art imagery is also exploited to gain academic capital. To exclude academic exploitation of rock art from commercial uses is to privilege archaeological exploitation of the cultural property of others. Much of the discussion centers on archaeologists' asserting their perceived rights to determine control of and access to rock art imagery without realizing that such claims are potentially as dubious as those wishing to profit from rock art by placing its imagery on popular material culture. The researcher who criticized "insensitive and unfaithful" reproductions of rock art imagery had such imagery reproduced on a series of notes and cards based on a series of tracings that "accurately capture[d] the outline and detail . . . of the image. But in a sense these re-reproductions are highly inaccurate. For instance, they downplay color" (Dowson 1999:5). In what sense can this appropriation of rock art imagery be any less sensitive than commercial uses that "destroy the meaning of the image" (Dowson 1999:5)?

It is important to ask (1) what is it that is actually being commodified? and (2) what is the role of archaeologists in the commodification of imagery?

First, what is actually being commodified? Foucault (1983 [1973]) uses Magritte's (1926) painting of a pipe with its legend "Ceci n'est pas une pipe" ("This is not a pipe") to highlight the fundamental gap between signifiers and things. Foucault discusses at least four possibilities regarding "meaning":

1. This is not a pipe but a drawing of a pipe.
2. This is not a pipe but a sentence saying that this is not a pipe.
3. The sentence "This is not a pipe" is not a pipe.
4. In the sentence "This is not a pipe," this is not a pipe: the painting, written sentence, drawing of a pipe—all this is not a pipe. (Foucault 1983 [1973])

The negations are numerous, and at no point can the image connect with the words. As Tilley (1990) notes, "In describing material culture we are producing discursive objects on which subsequent discourse may then set to work. At no point are we transparently dealing with the 'real.' "

We do not mistake a slide of a rock art image for the rock art itself; we understand it to be but a representation (or if one prefers, a simulacrum) of it. And all representations are imperfect and unable to fully capture the character of its referential subject. Yet, the circulation of rock art imagery in contemporary cultural media is controversial and bound up with issues of accuracy of reproduction. It is a general maxim in the anthropology of symbolism that any change in context changes the references and meanings of a symbol (Sperber 1975). Consequently, rock art imagery, when it is represented on mugs, slides, books, and so on, has its original meanings and connotations changed and ceases to function as rock art. It becomes an approximation of a real-world object, and is no more inaccurate for being depicted on a mug than in an academic book, since texture, size, and so on, as well as landscape context are not necessarily captured in either reproduction (or re-inscription).

The paradox is that archaeology's activities make possible the commercial exploitation of rock art (Welsh 1999). The pursuit of academic capital results in the publication of texts consumed by the archaeological community or the general public. Reports, research papers, site guides, and site documentation constitute a textual inscribing of rock art imagery that frees it from its landscape context. The collections of signifiers of imagery that accompany a final site report, or adorn the pages of a coffee table book, inscribe the site into a novel cultural text that is free to circulate with other cultural texts. It becomes capable of being used in a variety of discourses irrespective of the intentions of its author (both those who made the art and the archaeologists who wrote the report). The only way to prevent this process would be for archaeologists not to publish illustrative materials, and there seems little chance of this happening except in those cases where indigenous communities control the circulation of rock art imagery.

Yet this indignation about public consumption of rock art imagery takes place in a context of severe threats to the physical integrity of rock art sites and their locales, particularly in the western United States, where states such as Nevada are experiencing dramatic population growth (Woody et al. in press). At their most serious, these threats are manifested as direct commodification of rock art imagery, with rock art physically removed from its site context for sale, or destroyed by graffiti. Surprisingly, the response of rock art specialists to cases of theft or vandalism of rock art panels is not uniform, as evidenced after the theft of petroglyph boulders from Peavine, Reno, in September 2003. In the resulting trial of the thieves, two well-known rock art specialists—Ronald Dorn and David Whitley—testified on behalf of the defense; for more information, see the debate in Dorn (2005) and Woody (2005).

More complex is the conflict that arises when indigenous practices may affect the rock art heritage that archaeologists are seeking to protect, at the price of destroying the site's cultural value to its users. One of the best examples illustrating the complex issues involved comes from southern Kimberley, where the Australian federal government gave a grant for the Wanang

Ngari Aboriginal Corporation to train young unemployed people to repaint Wandjina rock paintings (Morwood 2002:301–5). Repainting is an important way of both renewing the cultural significance of rock art and teaching the novices traditional practices and beliefs (2002:303–4). The repainting project was halted after protests from a non-Aboriginal lessee about the low level of consultation with local Aboriginal people and the standard of the repainting. The controversy involved several issues, including whether only Aboriginals had the right to make decisions about the management of rock art sites, whether the repainting was a continuation of or a parody of the traditional system, whether the poor condition of the original paintings mitigated the effects of repainting, and whether unskilled novices should have been allowed to do the repainting. As Morwood comments, the indigenous communities did not have a consensus. The chairman of the Wanang Ngari Aboriginal Corporation strongly supported the repainting as a way of teaching Aborigines about their cultural heritage, but the Aboriginal owners of the land on which the repainting took place were concerned: "When these kids were brought from Derby we didn't know they were a painting crew and they just ruined all our paintings; we've got no decent paintings to take our kids for learning our law. We doing now our own law during the wet" (Billy King, quoted in Morwood 2002:304).

As Morwood (2002:304) observes, somewhat surprisingly the positive Aboriginal view of repainting prevailed in the academic community rather than the "negative" view, which was more in accord with archaeological notions of conservation.

Poor archaeological practice (or "professional vandalism," as Bednarik [2001:97] terms it) is responsible for site damage even where researchers seek to respect the perceived religious context of rock art sites. In Sweden, petroglyphs are painted with red acrylic paint as the final part of the recording process in order to restore the site to its perceived original state (it being believed that petroglyphs were originally in-filled with red pigment). Surprisingly, "research is being conducted into the longevity of different paints for this very purpose" (Bednarik 2001:97). Likewise, in some parts of the world researchers clean petroglyphs with wire brushes before recording; direct tracing of painted art is sometimes justified by the knowledge that "it's going to disappear sooner or later," leading one to wonder why sooner is better. One can even still occasionally find researchers who justify chalking because they use a "special" kind of chalk! Minimizing impacts to site integrity should be the goal of all researchers, and that is one important way in which we as outsiders can respect the original cultural significance of a site.

Much of the debate regarding public consumption of rock art imagery is insufficiently reflexive, as it omits consideration of archaeology's role in fostering the conditions necessary for the commodification of rock art. By stressing the perceived sacred nature of rock art, researchers give it a cultural value that resonates with public misperceptions of the "primitive piety" of non-Western peoples. This effect is greatly enhanced by a preference for interpretations stressing shamanism, since this configuration of religious practices has considerable appeal for Westerners and has been incorporated into the New Age movement as neo-shamanism or core-shamanism (Jakobsen 1999:chapter 4). Consequently, it is not surprising that rock art excites public interest, an interest that archaeological texts have helped to promote. By strongly opposing the circulation of imagery in Western cultural media, archaeologists forget that our labors produce the materials necessary (photographs, line drawings, and so on) for rock art imagery to become inscribed on the mugs and T-shirts that we criticize. Yet we forget that discourse always escapes the intentions of its author(s)—thus there seems to be little we can do about the public consumption of rock art imagery until such time as archaeologists agree upon a moratorium on photographing and drawing sites. However, the preservation of rock art sites unavoidably requires textual inscription, which frees imagery to circulate in, and with, other cultural texts. Complaining about the public uses of rock art imagery seems a trivial activity when sites are being destroyed through looting, unsupervised public access, and professional poor practice. More can be done to respect the physical integrity of sites and to ensure that future generations' experience of rock art will not be solely virtual or textual. Preserving site integrity is perhaps the most important way that professional researchers can respect and enhance rock art's original cultural significance and the wishes of the traditional custodians of the sites.

References

Adams, Jenny L.

1993 Mechanisms of wear on ground stone artifacts. *Pacific Coast Archaeological Society Quarterly* 29 (4): 61–74.

Agai-Ticutta (Walker River Paiute Tribe)

1977 Summer Extension Program. Unpublished pamphlet. Schurz, Nevada.

Aikens, C. Melvin, and Younger T. Witherspoon

1986 Great Basin Numic prehistory: Linguistics, archeology, and environment. In *Anthropology of the Desert West: Essays in honor of Jesse D. Jennings*, ed. Carol J. Condie and Don D. Fowler, 7–20. University of Utah Anthropological Papers, no. 110. Salt Lake City: University of Utah Press.

Anderson, E. W., M. M. Borman, and W. C. Krueger

1998 *The ecological provinces of Oregon: A treatise on the basic ecological geography of the state.* Corvallis, OR: Oregon Agricultural Experiment Station.

Anderson, Richard L.

1979 *Art in small scale societies.* 2d ed. Englewood Cliffs, NJ: Prentice Hall.

Andrefsky, W., Jr., and K. Presler

2000 *Archaeological investigations at Birch Creek (35ML181): 1998–99 interim report.* Contributions in Cultural Resource Management, no. 66. Pullman, WA: Center for Northwest Anthropology, Washington State University.

Antevs, Ernst

1948 *The Great Basin, with emphasis on glacial and post-glacial times; climatic changes and pre-white man.* Biological Series 10 (7), University of Utah Bulletin 38 (20). Salt Lake City: University of Utah.

Ashmore, Wendy

2004 Social archaeologies of landscape. In *A companion to social archaeology*, ed. Lynn Meskell and Robert W. Preucel, 255–71. Malden, MA: Blackwell.

Bahn, Paul G.

1988 Comments on *The signs of all times*, by J. D. Lewis-Williams and T. A. Dowson. *Current Anthropology* 29:217–18.

1991 Where's the beef? The myth of hunting magic in Palaeolithic art. In *Rock art and prehistory: Papers presented to Symposium G of the AURA Congress, Darwin 1988*, ed. Paul G. Bahn and Andrée Rosenfeld, 1–13. Oxbow Monograph 10. Oxford: Oxbow Books.

1998 Preface to *Coso rock art: A new perspective*, ed. Elva Younkin, ix–x. Ridgecrest, CA: Maturango Museum.

Bahn, Paul, and Jean Vertut
1997 *Journey through the Ice Age*. 2d ed. London: Weidenfeld and Nicholson.

Barrett, Samuel A.
1917 The Washo Indians. *Bulletin of the Public Museum of the City of Milwaukee* 2 (1). Milwaukee: Public Museum of the City of Milwaukee.

Bass, Patricia M.
1994 A gendered search through some West Texas rock art. In *New light on old art: Recent advances in hunter-gatherer rock art research*, ed. David S. Whitley and Lawrence L. Loendorf, 67–74. Los Angeles: Institute of Archaeology, University of California.

Basso, Keith H.
1996 *Wisdom sits in places: Landscape and language among the Western Apache*. Albuquerque: University of New Mexico Press.

Baumhoff, Martin A.
1980 The evolution of Pomo society. *Journal of California and Great Basin Anthropology* 2:175–86.

Baumhoff, Martin A., and D. L. Olmsted
1963 Palaihnihan: Radiocarbon support for glottochronology. *American Anthropologist* 65:278–84.

Beck, Charlotte, and George T. Jones
1997 The terminal Pleistocene/early Holocene archaeology of the Great Basin. *Journal of World Prehistory* 11:161–236.

Beck, W., D. J. Donahue, A. J. T. Jull, G. Burr, W. S. Broecker, G. Bonani, I. Hajdas, and E. Malotki
1998 Ambiguities in direct dating of rock surfaces using radiocarbon measurements. *Science* 280:2132–35.

Bednarik, Robert G.
1995 The Côa petroglyphs: An obituary to the stylistic dating of Palaeolithic rock-art. *Antiquity* 69:877–83.

2001 *Rock art science: The scientific study of palaeoart.* International Federation of Rock Art Organizations, vol. 1. Turnhout, Belgium: Brepols.

2002 The dating of rock art: A critique. *Journal of Archaeological Science* 29:1213–33.

Bedwell, Stephen

1970 Prehistory and environment of the pluvial Fort Rock Lake area of south-central Oregon. Ph.D. diss., University of Oregon, Eugene.

Bender, Barbara

1989 Theorizing landscapes. *Man* (N.S.) 27:735–55.

Benson, L. V., P. A. Meyers, and R. J. Spencer

1991 Change in the size of Walker Lake during the past 5000 years. *Palaeogeography, Palaeoclimatology, Palaeoecology* 81:189–214.

Bettinger, Robert L.

1991 *Hunter-gatherers: Archaeological and evolutionary theory.* New York: Plenum.

Bettinger, Robert L., and Martin A. Baumhoff

1982 The Numic spread: Great Basin cultures in competition. *American Antiquity* 47:485–503.

Bierman, Paul R., and Alan R. Gillespie

1991 Accuracy of rock-varnish chemical analysis: Implications for cation-ratio dating. *Geology* 19:196–99.

Bierman, Paul R., Alan R. Gillespie, and Scott Kuehner

1991 Precision of rock-varnish chemical analysis and cation-ratio ages. *Geology* 19:135–38.

Binford, Lewis R.

1980 Willow smoke and dogs' tails: Hunter-gatherer settlement systems and archaeological site formation. *American Antiquity* 45:4–20.

1981 *Bones, ancient men, and modern myth.* New York: Academic Press.

Blackburn, Thomas C.

1977 Biopsychological aspects of Chumash rock art. *Journal of California and Great Basin Anthropology* 4:88–94.

Bloch, Maurice

1995 Questions not to ask of Malagasy carvings. In *Finding meaning in the past,* ed. Ian Hodder, Michael Shanks, Alexandra Alexandri, Victor Buchli, John Carman, Jonathan Last, and Gavin Lucas, 212–15. London: Routledge.

Boreson, Keo

1998 Rock art. In *Plateau,* ed. Deward E. Walker, Jr., 611–19. Handbook of North American Indians, vol. 12, gen. ed. William C. Sturtevant. Washington, D.C.: Smithsonian Institution.

2002 *Art inventory and documentation in the Watson area, Owyhee Reservoir, southeastern Oregon.* Eastern Washington University Reports in Archaeology and History, no. 100–117. Cheney, WA: Archaeological and Historical Services.

Bourdieu, Pierre

1991 *Language and symbolic power.* Trans. G. Raymond and M. Adamson. Cambridge: Polity Press.

Bradbury, J. Platt, R. M. Forester, and Robert S. Thompson

1989 Late Quaternary paleolimnology of Walker Lake, Nevada. *Journal of Paleolimnology* 1:249–68.

Bradley, Richard

1993 *Altering the earth: The origins of monuments in Britain and Continental Europe.* The Rhind Lectures 1991–92. Edinburgh: Society of Antiquaries of Scotland.

1997 *Rock art and the prehistory of Atlantic Europe: Signing the land.* London: Routledge.

1998 *The significance of monuments: On the shaping of human experience in Neolithic and Bronze Age Europe.* London: Routledge.

2000 *An archaeology of natural places.* London: Routledge.

Breuil, Henri

1952 *Quatre cents siècles d'art pariétal.* Montignac, France: Centre d'Études et de Documentation Préhistoriques.

Bullen, Margaret

1991 An interpretation of images of women in the rock art of northern Australia. In *Rock art and prehistory: Papers presented to symposium G of the AURA Congress, Darwin 1988,* ed. Paul Bahn and Andrée Rosenfeld, 53–57. Oxbow Monograph 10. Oxford: Oxbow Books.

Cannon, William J.

1987 Long Lake field notes. Manuscript on file. Bureau of Land Management, Lake View, Oregon.

Cannon, William J., C. Clifford Creger, Don D. Fowler, Eugene M. Hattori, and Mary F. Ricks

1990 A wetlands and uplands settlement-subsistence for Warner Valley, Oregon. In *Wetlands adaptations in the Great Basin,* ed. Joel C. Janetski and David B.

Madsen, 173–82. Occasional Papers, no. 1. Salt Lake City: Museum of Peoples and Cultures, Brigham Young University.

Cannon, William J., and Mary F. Ricks
1986 The Lake County Oregon Rock Art Inventory: Implications for prehistoric settlement and land use patterns. In *Contributions to the archaeology of Oregon, 1983–1986*, ed. Kenneth M. Ames, 1–22. Department of Anthropology and University Foundation Occasional Papers, no. 3. Salem, OR: Portland State University and the Association of Oregon Archaeologists.
1999 Rock Art as an indicator of site age in the northern Great Basin. Paper presented at the 64th annual meeting of the Society for American Archaeology, Chicago.

Carmichael, David L., Jane Hubert, Brian Reeves, and Audhild Schanche, eds.
1994 *Sacred sites, sacred places.* London: Routledge.

Chaffee, Scott D., Marian Hyman, and Marvin W. Rowe
1993a AMS ^{14}C dating of rock paintings. In *Time and space: Dating and spatial considerations in rock art research,* ed. Jack Steinbring, Alan Watchman, Paul Faulstich, and Paul S. C. Taçon, 67–73. Occasional Publication no. 8. Melbourne: Australian Rock Art Research Association.
1993b Direct dating of pictographs. In *American Indian rock art,* vol. 19, ed. Frank G. Bock, 23–30. San Miguel, CA: American Rock Art Research Association.

Chippindale, Christopher, and Paul S. C. Taçon
1998 The many ways of dating Arnhem Land rock-art, North Australia. In *The archaeology of rock-art,* ed. Christopher Chippindale and Paul S. C. Taçon, 90–111. Cambridge: Cambridge University Press.

Christopherson, R. W.
1997 *Geosystems.* Upper Saddle River, NJ: Prentice Hall.

Clemmer, Richard O., L. Daniel Myers, and Mary E. Rudden, eds.
1999 *Julian Steward and the Great Basin: The making of an anthropologist.* Salt Lake City: University of Utah Press.

Clottes, Jean
1998a Paint analyses from several Magdalenian caves in the Ariege region of France. *Journal of Archaeological Science* 20:223–35.
1998b The "three Cs": Fresh avenues towards European Palaeolithic art. In *The archaeology of rock-art,* ed. Christopher Chippindale and Paul S. C. Taçon, 112–29. Cambridge: Cambridge University Press.

Clottes, Jean, and David Lewis-Williams
1998 *The shamans of prehistory: Trance and magic in the painted caves.* Trans. Sophie Hawkes. New York: Abrams.

Conkey, Margaret W.
1980 The identification of prehistoric hunter-gatherer aggregation sites: The case of Altamira. *Current Anthropology* 21:609–30.

Conkey, Margaret W., and J. Spector
1984 Archaeology and the study of gender. *Advances in Archaeological Method and Theory* 7:1–38.

Conner, Stuart, and Betty Lu Conner
1971 Rock art of the Montana High Plains. Exhibition catalog, the Art Galleries, University of California, Santa Barbara, April 6–May 15, 1971.

Connick, Robert E., and Francis Connick
1995 A summer solstice petroglyph site. In *Rock art studies in the Americas: Papers presented to Symposium B of the AURA Congress, Darwin, 1988,* ed. Jack Steinbring, 111–15. Oxford: Oxbow Books.

Cook, J. R., and S. G. Fulmer
1981 The archaeology of the McCain Valley study area in eastern San Diego County, California: A scientific Class II cultural resource inventory. Report submitted to the Bureau of Land Management, Riverside, California.

Couture, Marilyn D.
1978 Recent and contemporary foraging practices of the Harney Valley Paiute. Master's thesis, Portland State University, Portland, Oregon.

Couture, Marilyn D., Mary F. Ricks, and Lucile Housley
1986 Foraging behavior of a contemporary northern Great Basin population. *Journal of California and Great Basin Anthropology* 8:150–60.

Cressman, Luther S.
1937 *Petroglyphs of Oregon.* University of Oregon Monographs, Studies in Anthropology, no. 2. Eugene: University of Oregon.

Currie, L. A., J. D. Kessler, J. V. Marolf, A. P. McNichol, D. R. Stuart, J. C. Donoghue, D. J. Donahue, G. S. Burr, and D. Biddulph
2000 Low-level (submicromole) environmental ^{14}C metrology. *Nuclear Instruments and Methods in Physics Research Section B: Beam Interactions with Materials and Atoms* 172 (1–4): 440–48.

Curtis, Edward S.

1997 [1926] *The North American Indian: The complete portfolios.* Cologne: Taschen.

Davis, Whitney

1988 Comments on *The Signs of All Times,* by J. D. Lewis-Williams and T. A. Dowson. *Current Anthropology* 29:222–24.

d'Azevedo, Warren L.

1986 Washoe. In *Great Basin,* ed. Warren L. d'Azevedo, 466–98. Handbook of North American Indians, vol. 11, gen. ed. William C. Sturtevant. Washington, D.C.: Smithsonian Institution.

d'Azevedo, Warren L. (ed.)

1986 Great Basin. Handbook of North American Indians, vol. 11, gen. ed. William C. Sturtevant. Washington, D.C.: Smithsonian Institution.

Delacorte, Michael G.

1997 *Culture change along the eastern Sierra Nevada/Cascade front: Volume 7—Pah Rah Uplands.* Far Western Anthropological Research Group. Report submitted to the Bureau of Land Management, Carson District, Nevada.

Dixon, Roland B.

1905 The Northern Maidu. *Bulletin of the American Museum of Natural History,* 17 (3): 119–346. New York: American Museum of Natural History.

1912 Maidu texts. *Publications of the American Ethnological Society,* 4:1–241. Leyden, Holland.

Dorn, Ronald I.

1983 Cation-ratio dating: A new rock varnish age-determination technique. *Quaternary Research* 20:49–73.

1994a Dating petroglyphs with a three-tier rock varnish approach. In *New light on old art: Recent advances in hunter-gatherer rock art research,* ed. David S. Whitley and Lawrence L. Loendorf, 13–36. Los Angeles: Institute of Archaeology, University of California.

1994b Surface exposure dating with rock varnish. In *Dating in surface and exposed contexts,* ed. Charlotte Beck, 77–113. Albuquerque: University of New Mexico Press.

1996 A change of perception. *La Pintura* 23 (2): 10–11.

1997 Constraining the age of the Côa Valley (Portugal) engravings with radiocarbon dating. *Antiquity* 71:105–15.

1998a Age determination of the Coso rock art. In *Coso rock art: A new perspective,* ed. Elva Younkin, 69–96. Ridgecrest, CA: Maturango Museum Press.

1998b *Rock coatings*. Amsterdam: Elsevier.
2005 Why testify for the defense? *La Pintura* 31 (2): 8–12.

Dorn, Ronald I., and David S. Whitley
1984 Chronometric and relative age determination of petroglyphs in the western United States. *Annals of the Association of American Geographers* 74:308–22.

Douglas, Mary
1975 *Implicit meanings*. London: Routledge and Kegan Paul.

Dowson, Thomas A.
1999 Off the rocks, onto T-shirts, canvasses, etc. . . . Power and the popular consumption of rock art imagery. In *Rock art and ethics: A dialogue,* ed. William D. Hyder, 1–14. Occasional Paper no. 3. Tucson, AZ: American Rock Art Research Association.

Driver, Harold E.
1937 Culture element distributions: VI—Southern Sierra Nevada. *Anthropological Records* 1 (2): 53–154. Berkeley: University of California.

Dronfield, Jeremy
1996 The vision thing: Diagnosis of endogenous derivation in "abstract" arts. *Current Anthropology* 37:373–91.

Du Bois, Constance Goddard
1908 The religion of the Luiseño Indians of Southern California. *Publications in American Archaeology and Ethnology* 8 (3): 69–186. Berkeley: University of California.

Durkheim, Emile
1995 [1912] *The elementary forms of religious life*. Trans. Karen E. Fields. New York: Free Press.

Echo-Hawk, Roger C.
2000 Ancient history in the New World: Integrating oral traditions and the archaeological record in deep time. *American Antiquity* 65:267–90.

Elias, T. S., and P. A. Dykeman
1982 *Edible wild plants, A North American field guide*. New York: Sterling.

Elston, Robert G.
1971 *A contribution to Washo archaeology*. Nevada Archaeological Survey, Research Paper no. 2. Reno: University of Nevada.

1979 *The archaeology of US 395 right-of-way between Stead, Nevada, and Halle-lujah Junction, California*. Nevada Archaeology Survey. Reno: Department of Anthropology, University of Nevada.

Elston, Robert G., and David W. Zeanah
2002 Thinking outside the box: A new perspective on diet breadth and sexual division of labor in the Prearchaic Great Basin. *World Archaeology* 34:103–30.

Erwin, Richard P.
1930 Indian rock writing in Idaho. In *12th biennial report of the State Historical Society of Idaho for the years 1929–30*, 2:35–111. Boise: State Historical Society of Idaho.

Fagan, John L.
1974 *Altithermal occupation of spring sites in the Northern Great Basin*. University of Oregon Monographs, Anthropological Papers, no. 6. Eugene: University of Oregon.

Farber, Alfred
1982 *Archaeological excavations at the Chalk Bluff Ridge, Nevada County, California: With a new interpretation of the Martis and Mesilla complexes*. Research Archaeological Program Anthropological Papers, no. 3. Chico, CA: California State University.

Fitzgerald, R. T., and T. L. Jones
1999 The Milling Stone Horizon revisited: New perspectives from Northern and Central California. *Journal of California and Great Basin Anthropology* 21:67–93.

Foit, Franklin F.
1985 Volcanic ash samples. Letter report on file. Bureau of Land Management, Lakeview, Oregon.

Foster, M. K.
1996 Language and culture history of North America. In *Languages*, ed. I. Goddard, 64–110. Handbook of North American Indians, vol. 17, gen. ed. William C. Sturtevant. Washington, D.C.: Smithsonian Institution.

Foucault, Michel
1983 [1973] *This is not a pipe*. Trans. J. Harkness. Berkeley: University of California Press.

Fowler, Catherine S.
1992 *In the shadow of Fox Peak: An ethnography of the Cattail-Eater Northern Paiute People of Stillwater Marsh*. Washington, D.C.: U.S. Government Printing Office.

Fowler, Catherine S., and Sven Liljeblad

1986 Northern Paiute. In *Great Basin,* ed. Warren d'Azevedo, 435–65. Handbook of North American Indians, vol. 11, gen. ed. William C. Sturtevant. Washington, D.C.: Smithsonian Institution.

Francis, Julie E.

2001 Style and classification. In *Handbook of rock art research,* ed. David S. Whitley, 221–44. Walnut Creek, CA: Altamira Press.

Francis, Julie E., and Lawrence L. Loendorf

2002 *Ancient visions: Petroglyphs and pictographs of the Wind River and Bighorn Country, Wyoming and Montana.* Salt Lake City: University of Utah Press.

Frazer, James G.

1922 *The golden bough: A study in magic and religion.* Abridged ed. Vol. 1. London: Macmillan.

Gagnon, A. R., A. P. McNichol, J. C. Donoghue, D. R. Stuart, K. von Reden, and NOSAMS

2000 The NOSAMS sample preparation laboratory in the next millennium: Progress after the WOCE program. *Nuclear Instruments and Methods in Physics Research* B:409–15.

Garfinkel, Alan P.

1982 The identification of prehistoric aboriginal groups through the study of rock art. In *Pictographs of the Coso region: Analysis and interpretation of the Coso Painted Style,* ed. Robert A. Schiffman, David S. Whitley, Alan P. Garfinkel and Stephen B. Andrews, 67–111. Bakersfield College Publications in Archaeology, no. 11. Bakersfield, CA: Bakersfield College.

Gebhard, D.

1966 The shield motif in Plains rock art. *American Antiquity* 31:721–31.

Gellner, Ernest

1985 *Relativism and the social sciences.* Cambridge: Cambridge University Press.

Gero, Joan M. and Margaret W. Conkey, eds.

1991 *Engendering archaeology: Women and prehistory.* Oxford: Blackwell.

Giddens, Anthony

1984 *The constitution of society: Outline of the theory of structuration.* Cambridge, UK: Polity Press.

Godelier, Maurice

1986 *The making of great men: Male domination and power among the New Guinea Baruya.* Cambridge: Cambridge University Press.

Gombrich, E. H.
1998 [1950] *The story of art.* 16th ed. London: Phaidon.

Grant, Campbell
1967 *Rock art of the American Indian.* New York: Thomas Y. Crowell.
1980 The desert bighorn and aboriginal man. In *The desert bighorn: Its life history, ecology, and management,* ed. Gale Monson and Lowell Sumner, 7–39. Tucson: University of Arizona Press.

Grant, Campbell, James W. Baird, and Kenneth Pringle
1968 *Rock drawings of the Coso Range: An ancient sheep-hunting cult pictured in desert rock carvings.* China Lake, CA: Maturango Museum.

Green, Eileen M.
1987 A cultural ecological approach to the rock art of southern Nevada. Master's thesis, University of Nevada, Las Vegas.

Halverson, J.
1987 Art for art's sake in the Palaeolithic. *Current Anthropology* 28:63–89.
Harry, Karen G.
1995 Cation-ratio dating of varnished artifacts: Testing the assumptions. *American Antiquity* 60:118–30.

Hartley, Ralph J.
1992 *Rock art on the Northern Colorado Plateau: Variability in content and context.* Aldershot, UK: Avebury Press.

Hays-Gilpin, Kelley A.
2004 *Ambiguous images: Gender and rock art.* Walnut Creek, CA: Altamira Press.

Hedges, Ken
1976 Southern California rock art as shamanic art. In *American Indian rock art,* vol. 2, ed. Kay Sutherland, 126–38. El Paso, TX: American Rock Art Research Association.
1982 Great Basin rock art styles: A revisionist view. In *American Indian rock art,* vols. 7 and 8, ed. Frank G. Bock, 205–11. El Toro, CA: American Rock Art Research Association.
1985 Rock art portrayals of shamanic transformation and magical flight. In *Rock art papers,* vol. 2, ed. Ken Hedges, 83–94. San Diego Museum Papers, no. 18. San Diego: San Diego Museum of Man.
1987 Patterned body anthropomorphs and the concept of phosphenes in rock art. In *Rock art papers,* vol. 5, ed. Ken Hedges, 17–24. San Diego Museum Papers, no. 21. San Diego: San Diego Museum of Man.

2001 Traversing the great gray middle ground: An examination of shamanistic interpretation of rock art. In *American Indian rock art,* vol. 27, ed. Steven M. Freers and Alanah Woody, 123–36. Tucson, AZ: American Rock Art Research Association.

Heizer, Robert F.
1942 Massacre Lake Cave, Tule Lake Cave, and shore sites. In *Archaeological researches in the Northern Great Basin,* ed. Luther S. Cressman, 121–34. Carnegie Institution of Washington Publications, no. 534. Washington, D.C.: Carnegie Institution of Washington.

Heizer, Robert F., and Martin A. Baumhoff
1959 Great Basin petroglyphs and prehistoric game trails. *Science* 129:904–5.
1962 *Prehistoric rock art of Nevada and eastern California.* Berkeley: University of California Press.

Heizer, Robert F., and Albert B. Elsasser
1953 *Some archaeological sites and cultures of the central Sierra Nevada.* Reports of the University of California Archaeological Survey, no. 21, 26–30. Berkeley, CA: Department of Anthropology, University of California, Berkeley.

Hodder, Ian
1986 *Reading the past: Current approaches to interpretation in archaeology.* Cambridge: Cambridge University Press.

Hughes, Richard E.
1986 *Diachronic variability in obsidian procurement patterns in northeast California and south central Oregon.* University of California Publications in Anthropology, no. 17. Berkeley: University of California Press.

Hyder, William D.
1999 Preface to *Rock art and ethics: A dialogue,* ed. William D. Hyder, vii–ix. Occasional Paper no. 3. Tucson, AZ: American Rock Art Research Association.

Ingold, Timothy
1986 Territoriality and tenure: The appropriation of space in hunting and gathering societies. In *The appropriation of nature: Essays on human ecology and social relations,* ed. Timothy Ingold, 130–64. Manchester, UK: Manchester University Press.

Jakobsen, Merete Demant
1999 *Shamanism: Traditional and contemporary Approaches to the mastery of spirits and healing.* New York: Berghahn Books.

Jenkins, Dennis L.
2003 The grasshopper and the ant: Middle Holocene occupations and storage behavior at the Bowling Dune site in the Fort Rock Basin, Central Oregon. Manuscript on file. Museum of Natural History, University of Oregon, Eugene.

Jochim, Michael A.
1988 Optimal foraging and the division of labor. *American Anthropologist* 90:130–36.

Johnson, D. S.
1981 High Basin northeast and Spanish Springs archaeology: An archaeological reconnaissance of the High Basin Northeast Sludge Disposal Alternative Area. Report no. 16–82, CR3-616p, submitted to City of Reno.

Johnson, Edward C.
1975 *Walker River Paiutes: A tribal history.* Walker River Paiute Tribe, Schurz, Nevada.

Jones, J. Claude
1925 Geologic history of Lake Lahontan. In *Quaternary climates.* Carnegie Institution of Washington Publication no. 352. Washington, D.C.: Carnegie Institution of Washington.

Jones, Terry L.
1996 Mortars, pestles, and division of labor in prehistoric California: A view from Big Sur. *American Antiquity* 61:234–64.

Kehoe, Alice B.
2000 *Shamans and religion: An anthropological exploration in critical thinking.* Prospect Heights, IL: Waveland Press.
2002 Emerging trends versus the popular paradigm in rock art research. *Antiquity* 76:384–85.

Kelly, Isabel T.
1932 Ethnography of the Surprise Valley Paiute. *Publications in American Archaeology and Ethnography* 31 (3): 67–210. Berkeley, CA: Department of Anthropology, University of California.

Kent, Susan
1998 Invisible gender, invisible foragers: Hunter-gatherer spatial patterning and the South African archaeological record. In *Gender in African prehistory,* ed. Susan Kent, 39–67. Walnut Creek, CA: Altamira Press.

Keyser, James D.

1975 A Shoshonean origin for the Plains shield bearing warrior. *Plains Anthropologist* 20:207–15.

Keyser, James D., and David S. Whitley

2006 Sympathetic magic in western North American rock art. *American Antiquity* 71:3–26.

King, G. Q.

1978 The late Quaternary history of Adrian Valley, Lyon County, Nevada. Master's thesis, University of Utah, Salt Lake City.

Knack, Martha C., and Omer C. Stewart

1984 *As long as the rivers shall run: An economic history of the Pyramid Lake Indian Reservation.* Berkeley: University of California Press.

Kowta, Makoto

1969 *The Sayles Complex: A late milling stone assemblage from Cajon Pass and the ecological implications of its scraper planes.* University of California Publications in Anthropology, no. 6. Berkeley, CA: Department of Anthropology, University of California.

1988 *The archaeology and prehistory of Plumas and Butte counties, California: An introduction and interpretive model.* California Archaeological Site Inventory Northeast Information Center. Chico: California State University.

2000 Exploring the historicity of Maidu myths: A work in progress. Paper presented at the Anthropology Forum, California State University, Chico.

2001 Post-processualism, evolutionary ecology, the medieval drought, and Maidu mythology: A preliminary model. Paper presented at the 35th annual meeting of the Society for California Archaeology, Modesto.

Kroeber, Alfred L.

1955 Linguistic time depth results so far and their meaning. *International Journal of American Linguistics* 21:91–104.

Kuhn, Thomas S.

1962 *The structure of scientific revolutions.* Chicago: University of Chicago Press.

Laird, Carobeth

1974 Chemehuevi religious beliefs and practices. *Journal of California Anthropology* 1:19–25.

Lamb, Sydney M.

1958 Linguistic prehistory in the Great Basin. *International Journal of American Linguistics* 24:95–100.

Layton, Robert

1985 The cultural context of hunter-gatherer rock art. *Man* (N.S.) 20:434–553.

1988 Comments on *The Signs of All Times,* by J. D. Lewis-Williams and T. A. Dowson. *Current Anthropology* 29:226–27.

1991 *The anthropology of art.* 2d ed. Cambridge: Cambridge University Press.

1992 *Australian rock art: A new synthesis.* Cambridge: Cambridge University Press.

2000a Intersubjectivity and understanding rock art. *Australian Archaeology* 51:48–53.

2000b Shamanism, totemism, and rock art: *Les Chamanes de la Préhistoire* in the context of rock art research. *Cambridge Archaeological Journal* 10:169–86.

Layton, Thomas N.

1970 High rock archaeology: An interpretation of the prehistory of the northwest Great Basin. Ph.D. diss., Harvard University, Cambridge, Massachusetts.

1985 Invaders from the south? Archaeological discontinuities in the northwestern Great Basin. *Journal of California and Great Basin Anthropology* 7:183–201.

Leach, Melinda

1988 Subsistence intensification and settlement change among prehistoric hunters and gatherers of the northwestern Great Basin. Ph.D. diss., University of California, Los Angeles.

1999 In search of gender in Great Basin prehistory. In *Models for the millennium: Great Basin anthropology today,* ed. Charlotte Beck, 182–91. Salt Lake City: University of Utah Press.

Lee, Georgia and William D. Hyder

1990 Relative dating and the rock art of Lava Beds National Monument. *Proceedings of the Society for California Archaeology* 3:195–205.

Leen, Daniel

1988 An inventory of Hells Canyon rock art, vol. 1. Report submitted to U.S. Forest Service, Hells Canyon National Recreation Area, Enterprise, Oregon.

Levy, Richard S.

1979 The linguistic prehistory of Central California: Historical linguistics and cultural process. Unpublished manuscript.

Lewis, Ioan M.

1986 *Religion in context: Cults and charisma.* Cambridge: Cambridge University Press.

1989 *Ecstatic religion: A study of shamanism and spirit possession.* 2d ed. London: Routledge.

Lewis-Williams, J. David

1981 *Believing and seeing: Symbolic meaning in southern San rock paintings.* London: Academic Press.

1991 Wrestling with analogy: A methodological dilemma in Upper Palaeolithic art research. *Proceedings of the Prehistoric Society* 57:149–62.

1997 Harnessing the brain: Vision and shamanism in Upper Paleolithic Western Europe. In *Beyond art: Pleistocene image and symbol,* ed. Margaret W. Conkey, Olga Soffer, Deborah Stratmann, and Nina G. Jablonski, 321–42. Memoirs of the California Academy of Sciences no. 23. San Francisco: California Academy of Sciences.

1998 Quanto? The issue of "many meanings" in Southern African San rock art research. *South African Archaeological Bulletin* 53:86–97.

2002 *The mind in the cave: Consciousness and the origins of art.* London: Thames and Hudson.

Lewis-Williams, J. David, and Thomas A. Dowson

1988 The signs of all times: Entoptic phenomena in Upper Palaeolithic art. *Current Anthropology* 29:201–45.

1990 Through the veil: San rock paintings and the rock face. *South African Archaeological Bulletin* 45:5–16.

1994 Aspects of rock art research: A critical retrospective. In *Contested images: Diversity in Southern African rock art research,* ed. Thomas A. Dowson and J. David Lewis-Williams, 201–21. Johannesburg: Witwatersrand University Press.

Loendorf, Lawrence L.

1990 A dated rock art panel of shield bearing warriors in south central Montana. *Plains Archaeologist* 35:45–54.

1994 Traditional archaeological methods and their applications at rock art sites. In *New light on old art: Recent advances in hunter-gatherer rock art research,* ed. David S. Whitley and Lawrence E. Loendorf, 95–104. Los Angeles: Institute of Archaeology, University of California.

Loring, J. Malcolm, and Louise Loring

1983 *Pictographs and petroglyphs of the Oregon country.* Part 2, *Southern Oregon.* Los Angeles: Institute of Archaeology, University of California.

Luttrell, Charles T.

2000 *A report on a Class III cultural resources inventory at the U.S. Bureau of Reclamation's Lake Owyhee Reservoir, Malheur County, Oregon.* Eastern Washington University Reports in Archaeology and History, no. 100–96. Cheney, WA: Archaeological and Historical Services.

Madsen, David B., and David Rhode (eds).

1994 *Across the West: Human population movement and the expansion of the Numa.* Salt Lake City: University of Utah Press.

Mallery, Garrick

1893 Picture-writing of the American Indians. In *Tenth annual report of the Bureau of American Ethnology for the Years 1888–1889*, 3–822. Washington, D.C.: U.S. Government Printing Office.

Mason, Ronald J.

2000 Archaeology and Native American oral traditions. *American Antiquity* 65:239–66.

McGuire, Kelly R., and William R. Hildebrandt

1994 The possibilities of women and men: Gender and California Milling Stone Horizon. *Journal of California and Great Basin Anthropology* 16:41–59.

McLane, Alvin R.

1980 *Cultural Resources Inventory in Spanish Springs Valley, Washoe County, Nevada.* Social Sciences Technical Report 16. Submitted to Director of Public Works, City of Reno.

1999 Pah Rah Range High Basins (Dry Lakes) Petroglyph District, Washoe County. Manuscript.

Miller, Wick R.

1986 Numic languages. In *Great Basin*, ed. Warren L. d'Azevedo, 98–106. Handbook of North American Indians, vol. 11, gen. ed. William C. Sturtevant. Washington, D.C.: Smithsonian Institution.

Mithen, Steven J.

1988 To hunt or to paint: Animals and art in the Upper Paleolithic. *Man* (N.S.) 23:671–95.

Monteleone, Sue Ann

1993 Paintings of the Eleana Range and vicinity, southern Nevada. In *Rock art papers*, vol. 10, ed. Ken Hedges, 37–47. San Diego Museum Papers, no. 29. San Diego: San Diego Museum of Man.

1998 Great Basin rock art: Numic tradition or multicultural diversity? In *American Indian rock art*, vol. 22, ed. Steven M. Freers, 19–28. Tucson, AZ: American Rock Art Research Association.

Monteleone, Sue Ann, and Alanah Woody

1999 Changing light on the Cosos. In *American Indian rock art*, vol. 24, ed. Steven M. Freers, 57–68. Tucson, AZ: American Rock Art Research Association.

Moore, Henrietta L.

1986 *Space, text, and gender: An anthropological study of the Marakwet of Kenya.* Cambridge: Cambridge University Press.

Moratto, Michael J.

1984 *California archaeology.* New York: Academic Press.

Morrison, R., and Jonathan O. Davis

1964 Quaternary stratigraphy and archaeology of the Lake Lahontan area: A reassessment. Field Trip 13. Annual meeting of the Geological Society of American and Affiliated Societies, Reno, Nevada.

Morwood, M. J.

2002 *Visions from the past: The archaeology of Australian aboriginal art.* Washington, D.C.: Smithsonian Institution Press.

Murphy, Robert F, and Yolanda Murphy

1986 Northern Shoshone and Bannock. In *Great Basin,* ed. Warren L. d'Azevedo, 284–307. Handbook of North American Indians, vol. 11, gen. ed. William C. Sturtevant. Washington, D.C.: Smithsonian Institution.

Nissen, Karen M.

1982 Images from the past: An analysis of six western Great Basin petroglyph sites. Ph.D. diss., University of California, Berkeley.

1995 Pray for signs? Petroglyph research in the Western Great Basin, North America. In *Rock art studies in the Americas: Papers from the Darwin Rock Art Congress,* ed. Jack Steinbring, 67–75. Oxbow Monograph 45. Oxford: Oxbow Books.

O'Connell, James F.

1971 The archaeology and cultural ecology of Surprise Valley, northeastern California. Ph.D. diss., University of California, Berkeley.

1975 *The prehistory of Surprise Valley.* Ramona, CA: Ballena Press.

Olsen, William H., and Francis A. Riddell

1963 *The archaeology of the Western Pacific Railroad relocations, Oroville Project, Butte County, California.* Archaeological Report No. 7 (State of California, Department of Parks and Recreation, Division of Beaches and Parks). Sacramento: State of California, Division of Beaches and Parks.

Ouzman, Sven

1998 Towards a mindscape of landscape: Rock-art as expression of world-understanding. In *The archaeology of rock-art,* ed. Christopher Chippindale and Paul S. C. Taçon, 30–41. Cambridge: Cambridge University Press.

Owen, Roger C.

1965 The patrilocal band: A linguistic and culturally hybrid social unit. *American Anthropologist* 67:675–90.

Park, Willard Z.

1934 Paviotso shamanism. *American Anthropologist* 36:98–113.

1938 *Shamanism in western North America: A study in cultural relationships.* Evanston, IL: Northwestern University.

Payen, Louis A.

1966 Prehistoric rock art in the northern Sierra Nevada, California. Master's thesis, California State University, Sacramento.

Payen, Louis A., and Lyle R. Scott

1982 *An archaeological sample survey of the Hawley Lake area, Sierra County, California.* Cultural Resource Report No. 11. US Forest Service, Pacific Southwest Region, Nevada City, California: U.S. Forest Service, Pacific SW Region.

Pendegraft, Signa W.

2005 Ground stone and pecked rock: Results of the High Basins Archaeological Analysis. Paper presented at the 70th annual meeting of the Society for American Archaeology, Salt Lake City.

Plew, Mark G.

1976 Shield-bearing warrior motif petroglyphs from southwestern Idaho. *The Masterkey* 50:112.

Price, Neil, ed.

2001 *The archaeology of shamanism.* London: Routledge.

Quinlan, Angus R.

1993 Towards an archaeology of religion. Ph.D. diss., University of Southampton, Southampton.

2000a Interpreting Nevada's rock art: The balancing act between general theory and ethnography. *Nevada Archaeologist* 18:16–25.

2000b The ventriloquist's dummy: A critical review of shamanism and rock art in far western North America. *Journal of California and Great Basin Anthropology* 22:92–108.

2001 Smoke and mirrors: Rock art and shamanism in California and the Great Basin. In *Shamanism: Uses and abuses of a concept,* ed. Henri-Paul Francfort and Roberte N. Hamayon, 189–205. Bibliotheca Shamanistica, vol. 10. Budapest: Akadémiai Kiadó.

Quinlan, Angus R., and Alanah Woody

2001 Marking time at Lagomarsino: The competing perspectives of rock art studies. In *American Indian rock art,* vol. 27, ed. Steven M. Freers and Alanah
Woody, 211–20. Tucson, AZ: American Rock Art Research Association.

2003 Marks of distinction: Rock art and ethnic identification in the Great Basin.
American Antiquity 68:372–90.

Randolph, Joseph E.

2001 The aboriginal rock art of the Lake Owyhee Reservoir, Oregon. Master's thesis, University of Wisconsin, Milwaukee.

Raven, Christopher

1981 An archaeological survey of the proposed Cavalry Camp seeding at Massacre
Lake, Washoe County, Nevada. Report submitted to Bureau of Land Management, Surprise Field Office, Cedarville, California.

Ray, Verne F.

1940 Culture elements distributions: XXII plateau. *Publications in Anthropological
Records* 8 (2): 99–262. Berkeley: Department of Anthropology, University of
California.

Rector, Carol H.

1985 Rock art as hunting magic: Anthropological fact or fiction? In *Rock art papers,*
vol. 8, ed. Ken Hedges, 127–32. San Diego Museum Papers, no. 18. San Diego.

Reinach, S.

1903 L'art et la magie à propos des peintures et des gravures de l'Âge de Rennes.
L'Anthropologie 14:257–66.

Renfrew, A. Colin

1985 *The archaeology of cult: The sanctuary of Phylakopi.* London: Thames and
Hudson.

Ricks, Mary F.

1995 A survey and analysis of prehistoric rock art of the Warner Valley Region,
Lake County, Oregon. Ph.D. diss., Portland State University, Portland, Oregon.

1998 Reconnaissance of rock art locations and associated archaeological sites.
Manuscript. Bureau of Land Management, Surprise Field Office, Cedarville,
California.

Ricks, Mary F., and William J. Cannon

1993 A preliminary report on the Lake County, Oregon, Rock Art Inventory:
A data base for rock art research. In *American Indian rock art,* vol. 12, ed.

William D. Hyder, 93–106. San Miguel, CA: American Rock Art Research Association.

Ricoeur, Paul
1981 *Hermeneutics and the human sciences.* Cambridge: Cambridge University Press.

Riddell, Francis A., and William E. Pritchard
1971 Archaeology of the Rainbow Point Site (4-Plu-s94), Bucks Lake, Plumas County, California. In *Great Basin Anthropological Conference 1970: Selected papers,* ed. C. Melvin Aikens, 59–102. University of Oregon Anthropological Papers, no. 1. Eugene: University of Oregon.

Ritter, Dale W.
1961 X-ray petroglyph in Nevada. *Screenings* 10:4.
1965 Petroglyphs: A few outstanding sites. *Screenings* 14:1–4.

Ritter, Eric W.
1966 Reflections on obsidian hydration readings from Massacre Lake Area, Nevada. Manuscript on file. Department of Anthropology, University of California, Davis.
1994 Scratched rock art complexes in the Desert West: Symbols for socio-religious communication. In *New light on old art: Recent advances in hunter-gatherer rock art research,* ed. David S. Whitley and Lawrence L. Loendorf, 51–66. Los Angeles: Institute of Archaeology, University of California.
2002 The rationalist scientific method in rock art studies: The Serendipity Shelter, Nevada. In *American Indian rock art,* vol. 28, ed. Alanah Woody, 1–24. Tucson, AZ: American Rock Art Research Association.

Ritter, Eric W., and Brian W. Hatoff
1998 Figures for explanations: Scratched petroglyphs at the Pistone Site in western Nevada. In *Rock art studies in the Great Basin,* ed. Eric W. Ritter, 3–46. Salinas, CA: Coyote Press.

Ross, M. A.
2000 Test excavations at three mid-elevation rock art sites, Warner Valley, Oregon. Master's thesis, Washington State University, Pullman.

Rusco, Mary K.
1969a Report of archaeological investigations in the Spanish Springs Canyon area, Washoe County, Nevada. Submitted to the Nevada Archaeological Survey, Reno.
1969b Survey and excavation in Spanish Springs Canyon area, 1969. *Nevada Archaeological Survey Reporter* 3:5.

1981 The Spanish Springs Canyon and Upper Valleys archaeological project: Progress report. Appendix to Cultural Resources Report No. 16-99-2, CR3-616(P). Submitted to the City of Reno.

Russell, Israel C.
1885 Geological history of Lake Lahontan: A Quaternary lake of northwestern Nevada. *Monographs of the United States Geological Survey,* vol. 11. Washington, D.C.: Government Printing Office.

Schaafsma, Polly
1986 Rock art. In *Great Basin,* ed. Warren d'Azevedo, 215–26. Handbook of North American Indians, vol. 11, gen. ed. William C. Sturtevant. Washington, D.C.: Smithsonian Institution.
1994 Trance and transformation in the canyons: Shamanism and early rock art on the Colorado Plateau. In *Shamanism and rock art in North America,* ed. Solveig Turpin, 45–71. Special Publication 1. San Antonio, TX: Rock Art Foundation.

Schneider, J. S.
1993 Milling implements: Biases and problems in their use as indicators of prehistoric behavior and paleoenvironment. *Pacific Coast Archaeological Society Quarterly* 29 (4): 5–21.

Shipley, William, and Richard A. Smith
1979 The roles of cognation and diffusion in a theory of Maidun prehistory. *Journal of California and Great Basin Anthropology, Papers in Linguistics* 1:65–73.

Shock, Myrtle. P.
2002 Rock art and settlement in the Owyhee Uplands of southeastern Oregon. Bachelor of Philosophy thesis, University of Pittsburgh.

Skotnes, Pippa
1991 Rock art: Is there life after trance? *De Arte* 44:16–24.

Slusser, S.
1999 *Soil survey of Washoe County, Nevada, north part.* Parts 1 and 2. USDA Natural Resources Conservation Service in cooperation with USDI Bureau of Land Management and University of Nevada Agricultural Experiment Station, Washington, D.C.

Smith, Claire E.
1991 Female artists: The unrecognized factor in sacred rock art production. In *Rock art and prehistory: Papers presented to Symposium G of the AURA Congress, Darwin 1988,* ed. Paul Bahn and Andrée Rosenfeld, 45–52. Oxford: Oxbow Books.

Smith, S. D., R. K. Monson, and J. E. Anderson
1997 *Physiological ecology of North American desert plants.* New York: Springer.

Solomon, Anne
1992 Gender, representation, and power in San ethnography and rock art. *Journal of Anthropological Archaeology* 11:291–329.

Sparkman, Philip S.
1908 The culture of the Luiseño Indians. *Publications in American Archaeology and Ethnology* 8 (4): 187–234. Berkeley: University of California.

Spencer, W. Baldwin, and F. J. Gillen
1899 *The native tribes of Central Australia.* London: Macmillan.

Sperber, Dan
1975 *Rethinking symbolism.* Cambridge: Cambridge University Press.

Spier, Leslie
1930 Klamath ethnography. *Publications in American Archaeology and Ethnology* 30 (1): 1–338. Berkeley: University of California.

Steward, Julian H.
1929 Petroglyphs of California and adjoining states. *Publications in American Archaeology and Ethnology* 24 (2): 47–238. Berkeley: University of California.
1937 Petroglyphs of the United States. In *Annual report of the Board of Regents of the Smithsonian Institution for 1936,* 405–25. Publication 3405. Washington, D.C.: Smithsonian Institution.
1938 *Basin-Plateau aboriginal sociopolitical groups.* Bureau of American Ethnology Bulletin no. 120. Washington, D.C.: Smithsonian Institution.
1941 Culture element distributions: 13—Nevada Shoshoni. *Anthropological Records* 4 (2): 209–360. Berkeley: University of California.
1943 Culture element distributions: 23—Northern and Gosiute Shoshoni. *Anthropological Records* 8 (3): 263–392. Berkeley: University of California.

Stewart, Omer C.
1939 The Northern Paiute bands. *Anthropological Records* 2 (3): 127–49. Berkeley: University of California.
1941 Culture element distributions: 14—Northern Paiute. *Anthropological Records* 4 (3): 361–446. Berkeley: University of California.
1942 Culture element distributions: 18—Ute-Southern Paiute. *Anthropological Records* 6 (2): 231–356. Berkeley: University of California.
1966 Tribal distributions and boundaries in the Great Basin. In *The current status of anthropological research in the Great Basin,* vol. 1, ed. Warren L. d'Azevedo.

Reno: University of Nevada Desert Research Institute Social Sciences and Humanities Publications.

Strong, William D.

1929 Aboriginal society in Southern California. *Publications in American Archaeology and Ethnology* 26 (1): 1–358. Berkeley: University of California.

Taçon, Paul S. C.

1994 Socialising landscapes: The long-term implications of signs, symbols, and marks on the land. *Archaeology in Oceania* 29:117–29.

Taçon, Paul S. C., and Christopher Chippindale

1998 An archaeology of rock-art through informed methods and formal methods. In *The archaeology of rock-art,* ed. Christopher Chippindale and Paul S. C. Taçon, 1–10. Cambridge: Cambridge University Press.

Tilley, Christopher

1990 Michel Foucault: Towards an archaeology of archaeology. In *Reading material culture,* ed. Christopher Tilley, 281–347. Oxford: Blackwell.

1991 *Material culture and text: The art of ambiguity.* London: Routledge.

1994 *A phenomenology of landscape: Places, paths, and monuments.* Oxford: Berg.

Tobias, Nelle

1981 The Wees Bar Petroglyph Field, Southwestern Idaho. Report submitted to Idaho State Historic Preservation Office and Boise State University, Boise.

Tratebas, Alice M.

1999 The earliest petroglyph traditions on the North American plains. In *Dating and the earliest known rock art: Papers presented in Symposia 1–3 of the SIARB Congress, Cochabamba, Bolivia, April 1997,* ed. Matthias Strecker and Paul Bahn, 15–28. Oxford: Oxbow Books.

True, Delbert L., Martin A. Baumhoff, and J. E. Hellen

1979 Millingstone cultures in Northern California: Berryessa I. *Journal of California and Great Basin Anthropology* 1:124–54.

Tuan, Yi-Fu

1977 *Space and place: The perspective of experience.* London: Arnold.

Tuohy, Donald R.

1963 Archaeological survey in southwestern Idaho and northern Nevada. *Nevada State Museum Anthropological Papers,* no. 8. Carson City: Nevada State Museum.

1969 A "wounded elephant" and three other petroglyphs in northern Washoe County, Nevada. *Nevada Archaeological Survey Reporter* 3:9–11.

1983 The treasure of the Sierra Madre . . . in the Wassuk Range? *Nevada Archaeological Survey Reporter* 12:1–11.
1985 Notes on the Great Basin distribution of Clovis Fluted and Folsom projectile points. *Nevada Archaeologist* 5:15–18.

Turner, Victor W.
1967 *The forest of symbols.* Ithaca, NY: Cornell University Press.

Turpin, Solveig A.
1994 On a wing and a prayer: Flight metaphors in Pecos River art. In *Shamanism and rock art in North America,* ed. Solveig A. Turpin, 73–102. Special Publication 1. San Antonio, TX: Rock Art Foundation.

Ucko, Peter J., and Robert Layton, eds.
1999 *The archaeology and anthropology of landscape: Shaping your landscape.* London: Routledge.

U.S. Bureau of Reclamation
1994 *Owyhee Reservoir resource management plan.* Pacific Northwest Region Bureau of Reclamation, Central Snake Projects Office. Boise, Idaho.

USDI Bureau of Land Management
1981 Lakeview grazing management draft environmental impact statement. Eugene, Oregon.

Vinnicombe, Patricia
1976 *People of the eland: Rock paintings of the Drakensberg bushmen as a reflection of their life and thought.* Pietermaritzburg, South Africa: Natal University Press.

Wallace, William J.
1955 A suggested chronology for Southern California coastal archaeology. *Southwestern Journal of Anthropology* 11:214–30.

Warren, Claude N.
1968 Cultural tradition and ecological adaptation on the Southern California coast. *Eastern New Mexico University Contributions to Anthropology* 1 (3): 1–14. Portales.

Watchman, Alan
1992 Doubtful dates for Karolta engravings. *Australian Aboriginal Studies* 1:51–55.
1993a More information about South Australian cation-ratio dates. *Rock Art Research* 10:40.
1993b Perspectives and potentials for absolute dating prehistoric rock paintings. *Antiquity* 67:58–65.

1995 Recent petroglyphs, Foz Côa, Portugal. *Rock Art Research* 12:104–8.

1997 Difference of interpretations for Foz Côa dating results. *Newsletter of the National Pictographic Society* 8:7.

1999 A review of the history of dating rock varnishes. *Earth-Science Reviews* 49:261–77.

Watchman, Alan, and Alanah Woody

2002 Dating rock varnishes associated with petroglyphs in Nevada. Paper presented at the 67th annual meeting of the Society for American Archaeology, Denver, Colorado.

Watchman, Alan, R. Lessard, A. J. T. Jull, L. J. Toolin, and W. Blake, Jr.

1993 14C Dating of laser-oxidized organics. *Radiocarbon* 35:331–35.

Watson, Patty Jo, and Mary C. Kennedy

1991 The development of horticulture in the eastern woodlands of North America: Women's role. In *Engendering Archaeology,* ed. Joan M. Gero and Margaret W. Conkey, 255–75. Oxford: Blackwell.

Weide, Margaret L.

1968 Cultural ecology of lakeside adaptations in the western Great Basin. Ph.D. diss., University of California, Los Angeles.

Wellmann, Klaus F.

1979 *Die Amerikanischen Felsbilder: American rock paintings and petroglyphs. A survey of North American Indian rock art.* Graz, Austria: Akademische Druck-u. Verlagsanstalt.

Welsh, Peter H.

1999 Commodification of rock art: An inalienable paradox. In *Rock art and ethics: A dialogue,* ed. William D. Hyder, 29–37. Occasional Paper no. 3. Tucson, AZ: American Rock Art Research Association.

Western Regional Climate Center

2005 Rome (Oregon) Weather Station climate data. Desert Research Institute, University of Nevada, Reno, Web page.

Wheat, Margaret

1967 *Survival arts of the primitive Paiutes.* Reno: University of Nevada Press.

Whistler, Kenneth W.

1977 Wintun prehistory: An interpretation based on linguistic reconstruction of plant and animal nomenclature. In *Proceedings of the third annual meeting of the Berkeley Linguistics Society.* Berkeley: Berkeley Linguistics Society.

Whiting, Beatrice B.

1950 *Paiute sorcery.* Viking Fund Publications in Anthropology, no. 15. New York: Viking Fund.

Whitley, David S.

1982 Notes on the Coso petroglyphs, the etiological mythology of the Western Shoshone, and the interpretation of rock art. *Journal of California and Great Basin Anthropology* 4:262–72.

1987 Socioreligious context and rock art in east-central California. *Journal of Anthropological Archaeology* 6:159–88.

1992 Shamanism and rock art in far western North America. *Cambridge Archaeological Journal* 2:89–113.

1994a By the hunter, for the gatherer: Art, social relations and subsistence change in the prehistoric Great Basin. *World Archaeology* 25:357–73.

1994b Ethnography and rock art in the far West: Some archaeological implications. In *New light on old art,* ed. David S. Whitley and Lawrence L. Loendorf, 81–93. Los Angeles: Institute of Archaeology, University of California.

1994c Shamanism, natural modeling, and the rock art of far western North American hunter gatherers. In *Shamanism and rock art in North America,* ed. Solveig A. Turpin, 1–43. Special Publication I. San Antonio: Rock Art Foundation.

1998a Finding rain in the desert: Landscape, gender, and far western North American rock-art. In *The archaeology of rock-art,* ed. Christopher Chippindale and Paul S. C. Taçon, 11–29. Cambridge: Cambridge University Press.

1998b *Following the shaman's path: A walking guide to Little Petroglyph Canyon, Coso Range, California.* Ridgecrest, CA: Maturango Press.

1998c Meaning and metaphor in the Coso petroglyphs: Understanding Great Basin rock art. In *Coso rock art: A new perspective,* ed. Elva Younkin, 109–74. Ridgecrest, CA: Maturango Press.

2000a *The art of the shaman: Rock art of California.* Salt Lake City: University of Utah Press.

2000b Reply to Quinlan. *Journal of California and Great Basin Anthropology* 22:108–29.

2000c Use and abuse of ethnohistory in the far West. In *1999 International Rock Art Congress proceedings.* Vol. 1. *Papers presented at the Twelfth International Rock Art Congress, Ripon, Wisconsin,* ed. Peggy Whitehead and Lawrence Loendorf, 127–53. Tucson, AZ: American Rock Art Research Association.

2003 What is Hedges arguing about? In *American Indian rock art,* vol. 29, ed. Alanah Woody, Joe T. O'Connor, and Anne McConnell, 83–104. Tucson, AZ: American Rock Art Research Association.

Whitley, David S., James Baird, Jean Bennett, and Robert G. Tuck
1984 The use of relative repatination in chronological ordering of petroglyph assemblages. *New World Archaeology* 6:19–25.

Wigand, Peter E.
1987 Diamond Pond, Harney County, Oregon: Vegetation history and water table in the Eastern Oregon desert. *Great Basin Naturalist* 47:427–58.

Woody, Alanah
1997a *Layer by layer: A multigenerational analysis of the Massacre Lake rock art site.* Department of Anthropology Technical Report 97-1. University of Nevada, Reno.
1997b Tired Dam—Report of excavations and survey conducted by the University of Nevada, Reno, 1994–1995. Prepared by the Department of Anthropology, University of Nevada, Reno. Report submitted to Bureau of Land Management, Lakeview, Oregon.
2000a How to do things with petroglyphs: The power of place in Nevada, USA. Ph.D. diss., University of Southampton, Southampton.
2000b Linking past and place: The construction and maintenance of tradition. In *International Rock Art Congress proceedings.* Vol. 1. *Papers presented at the Twelfth International Rock Art Congress, Ripon, Wisconsin,* ed. Peggy White-head and Lawrence L. Loendorf, 169–78. Tucson, AZ: American Rock Art Research Association.
2005 Reply to Dorn. *La Pintura* 31 (2): 12–14.

Woody, Alanah, Angus R. Quinlan, Cheryln Bennett, and Ralph Bennett
In press The Lagomarsino Canyon petroglyph site documentation project: The challenges of protecting and recording endangered rock art sites in a multi-use area. In *Proceedings of the Tenth International Rock Art Congress/RASI 2004, Agra, India,* ed. Robert G. Bednarik. Brussels: IFRAO.

Young, M. Jane
1988 *Signs from the ancestors: Zuni cultural symbolism and perceptions of rock art.* Publications of the American Folklore Society. Albuquerque: University of New Mexico Press.

Zilhão, João
1995 The stylistically Palaeolithic petroglyphs of the Côa valley, Portugal: A refutation of their "direct dating" to recent times. *Antiquity* 69:883–901.
2003 The Côa Valley: Research and management of a world heritage rock art site. *Rock Art Research* 20:53–68.

Contributors

Keo Boreson, Archaeological and Historical Services, Eastern Washington
   University, Cheney
Melvin Brown, Walker River Paiute Tribe, Schurz, Nevada
William J. Cannon, USDI Bureau of Land Management, Lakeview, Oregon
Farrell Cunningham, Maidu Cultural and Development Group
Signa W. Pendegraft, Department of Anthropology, University of Nevada, Reno
Angus R. Quinlan, Nevada Rock Art Foundation, Reno, and Summit Enviro-
   solutions, Carson City
Mary F. Ricks, Research Associate Professor Emerita, Portland State University,
   Beaverton, Oregon
Eric W. Ritter, USDI Bureau of Land Management, Redding, California
Myrtle P. Shock, Department of Anthropology, University of California, Santa
   Barbara
Helen Valborg, Blairsden, California
Alan Watchman, Consulting Geoscientist, Montrose, Colorado
Alanah Woody, Nevada Rock Art Foundation, Reno, and Nevada State Museum,
   Carson City

Index

Page numbers in italics refer to illustrations and tables.

Great Basin Carved Abstract, 132–33; repatination, 132–33; varnish samples, 133–36, *136*

McCain Valley (Calif.), 54–55

McLane, Alvin, 59

Mesilla Complex, 21, 22

Milling Stone Horizon, 21, 66

milling stones, *47, 48*. See also ground stone monuments: reuse of, 41, 57, 118, 126

Morwood, M., 148

Mountain Maidu. See Maidu

Mount Mazama, 114, 115, 131

Narrows site (Ore.), 47–48

Nisenan. See Maidu

Northern Paiute, *6,* 76, 93; ethnography, of 109–11; Fish Lake Eaters, 129; Harney Valley, Paiute 110–11; milling stone technology, 46; Numic dispersal, 129–30; shamanic power, acquisition of, 110; shamanism, 43, 48, 49, 110; Surprise Valley Paiute, 109–10; Tasiget-Tiviwari, 58; vision-quest locales, 43, 48, 49; Walker River Paiute, 11–12, 15–16

Northern Shoshone, 76, 93

Numic dispersal, 41, 42, 76, 109, 122, 123, 127, 129–30

Onkoito, the Age of, 29–30

oral tradition, 11, 42. See also ethnography

Owyhee Reservoir (Ore.) (Site 35ML1019), 93, *96, 97;* history of research, 94; imagery depicted, *98,* 98–103, *104;* styles of rock art, 95–97, 103–4, 106; stylistic elements of rock art, 97–103, *98, 99, 100–101, 102;* survey methods, 94–95

Owyhee uplands (Ore.): associated settlement archaeology, 79, *82,* 83–87, 90–91; history of archaeological research, 76–77; site contexts, 85–87, *87;* site 35ML1044, 83–85, *84;* spatial distribution of rock art sites, 79, *80,* 81, 84, 90; styles of rock art, *86,* 87–89, *88,*

90; survey methods, 78–79; vegetation, 77–78

Pah Rah Range. See High Basins (Nev.)

Paiute. See Northern Paiute

Peavine (Nev.), 147

Penutian: dispersal of, 22, 26, 27–28, 30

Pinto Complex, 21

Plumas County (Calif.): archaeology of, 21–22, 24–25; rock art styles, 23–24

"professional vandalism," 148–49

Reinach, S., 142, 143

religion: hunter-gatherer, 143–44, 145; origins of, 142–43. See also shamanism

repainting, 147–48

repatination, 134; of Great Basin Carved Abstract style, 121, 123, 132, 133

Ritter, Eric, 132

rock art: androcentrism in interpretation, 37–40, 49–50, 64–65, 67; archaeological neglect of, 45, 50, 52, 53, 112; art for art's sake, 143; associated with settlement archaeology, 3, 4, 6–7, 38, 42–49, 54–55, 59, *59, 60,* 61, *62, 63, 64,* 79, *80,* 83–87, 90–91, 112, 114, 116, 119, 122–23, 133–34; assumed ritual character of, 140–41, 142, 143; context and meaning of, 39, 50, 52–54, 63, 67–69, 71–75, 83, 89–90, 92–93, 118, 124; defined, 2; ethnography and interpretation of, 5, 71–72, 107, 117–18, 124, 142–43; formal methods of understanding, 71, 123–24; historic, 116–117, 118; history of research, 1–2; and identity, 23–24, 65, 67; in popular culture, 144–45, 149; stereotypes, 143–44, 145; temporal distancing from settlement archaeology, 57, 61, 63–64, 67, 118. See also styles, Great Basin rock art

Rusco, Mary, 61

Sage Hen Springs (Nev.), 133

Serpent Rock. See Agai-Pah Sea Serpent